Colloquies on Society

By

Robert Southey

The Echo Library 2006

Published by

The Echo Library

Echo Library
131 High St.
Teddington
Middlesex TW11 8HH

www.echo-library.com

Please report serious faults in the text to complaints@echo-library.com

ISBN 1-40683-002-X

INTRODUCTION

IT was in 1824 that Robert Southey, then fifty years old, published "Sir Thomas More, or Colloquies on the Progress and Prospects of Society," a book in two octavo volumes with plates illustrating lake scenery. There were later editions of the book in 1829, and in 1831, and there was an edition in one volume in 1837, at the beginning of the reign of Queen Victoria.

These dialogues with a meditative and patriotic ghost form separate dissertations upon various questions that concern the progress of society. Omitting a few dissertations that have lost the interest they had when the subjects they discussed were burning questions of the time, this volume retains the whole machinery of Southey's book. It gives unabridged the Colloquies that deal with the main principles of social life as Southey saw them in his latter days; and it includes, of course, the pleasant Colloquy that presents to us Southey himself, happy in his library, descanting on the course of time as illustrated by the bodies and the souls of books. As this volume does not reproduce all the Colloquies arranged by Southey under the main title of "Sir Thomas More," it avoids use of the main title, and ventures only to describe itself as "Colloquies on Society, by Robert Southey."

They are of great interest, for they present to us the form and character of the conservative reaction in a mind that was in youth impatient for reform. In Southey, as in Wordsworth, the reaction followed on experience of failure in the way taken by the revolutionists of France, with whose aims for the regeneration of Europe they had been in warmest accord. Neither Wordsworth nor Southey ever lowered the ideal of a higher life for man on earth. Southey retains it in these Colloquies, although he balances his own hope with the questionings of the ghost, and if he does look for a crowning race, regards it, with Tennyson, as a

"FAR OFF divine event
To which the whole Creation moves."

The conviction brought to men like Wordsworth and Southey by the failure of the French Revolution to attain its aim in the sudden elevation of society was not of vanity in the aim, but of vanity in any hope of its immediate attainment by main force. Southey makes More say to himself upon this question (page 37), "I admit that such an improved condition of society as you contemplate is possible, and that it ought always to be kept in view; but the error of supposing it too near, of fancying that there is a short road to it, is, of all the errors of these times, the most pernicious, because it seduces the young and generous, and betrays them imperceptibly into an alliance with whatever is flagitious and detestable." All strong reaction of mind tends towards excess in the opposite direction. Southey's detestation of the excesses of vile men that brought shame upon a revolutionary movement to which some of the purest hopes of earnest youth had given impulse, drove him, as it drove Wordsworth, into dread of everything that sought with passionate energy immediate change of evil into good. But in his own way no man ever strove more patiently than Southey to make evil good; and in his own home and his own life he gave good reason to one to whom he was as a father, and who knew his daily thoughts and deeds, to speak of him as "upon the whole the best man I have ever known."

In the days when this book was written, Southey lived at Greta Hall, by Keswick, and had gathered a large library about him. He was Poet Laureate. He had a pension from the Civil List, worth less than 200 pounds a year, and he was living at peace upon a little income enlarged by his yearly earnings as a writer. In 1818 his whole private fortune was 400 pounds in consols. In 1821 he had added to that some savings, and gave all to a ruined friend who had been good to him in former years. Yet in those days he refused an offer of 2,000 pounds a year to come to London and write for the Times. He was happiest in his home by Skiddaw, with his books about him and his wife about him.

Ten years after the publishing of these Colloquies, Southey's wife, who had been, as Southey said, "for forty years the life of his life," had to be placed in a lunatic asylum. She returned to him to die, and then his gentleness became still gentler as his own mind failed. He died in 1843. Three years before his death his friend Wordsworth visited him at Keswick, and was not recognised. But when Southey was told who it was, "then," Wordsworth wrote, "his eyes flashed for a moment with their former brightness, but he sank into the state in which I had found him, patting with both his hands his books affectionately, like a child."

Sir Thomas More, whose ghost communicates with Robert Southey, was born in 1478, and at the age of fifty-seven was beheaded for fidelity to conscience, on the 6th of July, 1535. He was, like Southey, a man of purest character, and in 1516, when his age was thirty-eight, there was published at Louvain his "Utopia," which sketched wittily an ideal commonwealth that was based on practical and earnest thought upon what constitutes a state, and in what direction to look for amendment of ills. More also withdrew from his most advanced post of opinion. When he wrote "Utopia" he advocated absolute freedom of opinion in matters of religion; in after years he believed it necessary to enforce conformity. King Henry VIII., stiff in his own opinions, had always believed that; and because More would not say that he was of one mind with him in the matter of the divorce of Katherine he sent him to the scaffold.

H. M.

COLLOQUY I

THE INTRODUCTION

"Posso aver certezza, e non paura,
Che raccontando quel che m' e accaduto,
Il ver diro, ne mi sara creduto."
"Orlando Innamorato," c. 5. st. 53.

It was during that melancholy November when the death of the Princess Charlotte had diffused throughout Great Britain a more general sorrow than had ever before been known in these kingdoms; I was sitting alone at evening in my library, and my thoughts had wandered from the book before me to the circumstances which made this national calamity be felt almost like a private affliction. While I was thus musing the post-woman arrived. My letters told me there was nothing exaggerated in the public accounts of the impression which this sudden loss had produced; that wherever you went you found the women of the family weeping, and that men could scarcely speak of the event without tears; that in all the better parts of the metropolis there was a sort of palsied feeling which seemed to affect the whole current of active life; and that for several days there prevailed in the streets a stillness like that of the Sabbath, but without its repose. I opened the newspaper; it was still bordered with broad mourning lines, and was filled with details concerning the deceased Princess. Her coffin and the ceremonies at her funeral were described as minutely as the order of her nuptials and her bridal dress had been, in the same journal, scarce eighteen months before. "Man," says Sir Thomas Brown, "is a noble animal, splendid in ashes, and pompous in the grave; solemnising nativities and deaths with equal lustre, nor omitting ceremonies of bravery in the infamy of his nature." These things led me in spirit to the vault, and I thought of the memorable dead among whom her mortal remains were now deposited. Possessed with such imaginations I leaned back upon the sofa and closed my eyes.

Ere long I was awakened from that conscious state of slumber in which the stream of fancy floweth as it listeth by the entrance of an elderly personage of grave and dignified appearance. His countenance and manner were remarkably benign, and announced a high degree of intellectual rank, and he accosted me in a voice of uncommon sweetness, saying, "Montesinos, a stranger from a distant country may intrude upon you without those credentials which in other cases you have a right to require." "From America!" I replied, rising to salute him. Some of the most gratifying visits which I have ever received have been from that part of the world. It gives me indeed more pleasure than I can express to welcome such travellers as have sometimes found their way from New England to those lakes and mountains; men who have not forgotten what they owe to their ancient mother; whose principles, and talents, and attainments would render them an ornament to any country, and might almost lead me to hope that their republican constitution may be more permanent than all other considerations would induce me either to suppose or wish.

"You judge of me," he made answer, "by my speech. I am, however, English by birth, and come now from a more distant country than America, wherein I have long been naturalised." Without explaining himself further, or allowing me time to make the inquiry which would naturally have followed, he asked me if I were not thinking of the Princess Charlotte when he disturbed me. "That," said I, "may easily be divined. All persons whose hearts are not filled with their own grief are thinking of her at this time. It had just occurred to me that on two former occasions when the heir apparent of England was cut off in the prime of life the nation was on the eve of a religious revolution in the first instance, and of a political one in the second."

"Prince Arthur and Prince Henry," he replied. "Do you notice this as ominous, or merely as remarkable?"

"Merely as remarkable," was my answer. "Yet there are certain moods of mind in which we can scarcely help ascribing an ominous importance to any remarkable coincidence wherein things of moment are concerned."

"Are you superstitious?" said he. "Understand me as using the word for want of a more appropriate one—not in its ordinary and contemptuous acceptation."

I smiled at the question, and replied, "Many persons would apply the epithet to me without qualifying it. This, you know, is the age of reason, and during the last hundred and fifty years men have been reasoning themselves out of everything that they ought to believe and feel. Among a certain miserable class, who are more numerous than is commonly supposed, he who believes in a First Cause and a future state is regarded with contempt as a superstitionist. The religious naturalist in his turn despises the feebler mind of the Socinian; and the Socinian looks with astonishment or pity at the weakness of those who, having by conscientious inquiry satisfied themselves of the authenticity of the Scriptures, are contented to believe what is written, and acknowledge humility to be the foundation of wisdom as well as of virtue. But for myself, many, if not most of those even who agree with me in all essential points, would be inclined to think me superstitious, because I am not ashamed to avow my persuasion that there are more things in heaven and earth than are dreamt of in their philosophy."

"You believe, then, in apparitions," said my visitor.

Montesinos.—Even so, sir. That such things should be is probable a priori; and I cannot refuse assent to the strong evidence that such things are, nor to the common consent which has prevailed among all people, everywhere, in all ages a belief indeed which is truly catholic, in the widest acceptation of the word. I am, by inquiry and conviction, as well as by inclination and feeling, a Christian; life would be intolerable to me if I were not so. "But," says Saint Evremont, "the most devout cannot always command their belief, nor the most impious their incredulity." I acknowledge with Sir Thomas Brown that, "as in philosophy, so in divinity, there are sturdy doubts and boisterous objections, wherewith the unhappiness of our knowledge too nearly acquainteth us;" and I confess with him that these are to be conquered, "not in a martial posture, but on our knees."

If then there are moments wherein I, who have satisfied my reason, and possess a firm and assured faith, feel that I have in this opinion a strong hold, I cannot but perceive that they who have endeavoured to dispossess the people of their old instinctive belief in such things have done little service to individuals and much injury to the community.

Stranger.—Do you extend this to a belief in witchcraft?

Montesinos.—The common stories of witchcraft confute themselves, as may be seen in all the trials for that offence. Upon this subject I would say with my old friend Charles Lamb -

"I do not love to credit tales of magic!
Heaven's music, which is order, seems unstrung.
And this brave world
(The mystery of God) unbeautified,
Disordered, marred, where such strange things are acted."

The only inference which can be drawn from the confession of some of the poor wretches who have suffered upon such charges is, that they had attempted to commit the crime, and thereby incurred the guilt and deserved the punishment. Of this indeed there have been recent instances; and in one atrocious case the criminal escaped because the statute against the imaginary offence is obsolete, and there exists no law which could reach the real one.

Stranger.—He who may wish to show with what absurd perversion the forms and technicalities of law are applied to obstruct the purposes of justice, which they were designed to further, may find excellent examples in England. But leaving this allow me to ask whether you think all the stories which are related of an intercourse between men and beings of a superior order, good or evil, are to be disbelieved like the vulgar tales of witchcraft

Montesinos.—If you happen, sir, to have read some of those ballads which I threw off in the high spirits of youth you may judge what my opinion then was of the grotesque demonology of the monks and middle ages by the use there made of it. But in the scale of existences there may be as many orders above us as below. We know there are creatures so minute that without the aid of our glasses they could never have been discovered; and this fact, if it were not notorious as well as certain, would appear not less incredible to sceptical minds than that there should be beings which are invisible to us because of their subtlety. That there are such I am as little able to doubt as I am to affirm anything concerning them; but if there are such, why not evil spirits, as well as wicked men? Many travellers who have been conversant with savages have been fully persuaded that their jugglers actually possessed some means of communication with the invisible world, and exercised a supernatural power which they derived from it. And not missionaries only have believed this, and old travellers who lived in ages of credulity, but more recent observers, such as Carver and Bruce, whose testimony is of great weight, and who were neither ignorant, nor weak, nor credulous men. What I have read concerning ordeals also staggers me; and I am sometimes inclined to think it more possible that when there has been full faith on all sides these appeals to divine justice may have been answered by Him who sees the secrets of all hearts than that modes of trial should have prevailed so long and so generally, from some of which no person could ever have escaped without an interposition of Providence. Thus it has appeared to me in my calm and unbiassed judgment. Yet I confess I should want faith to make the trial. May it not be, that by such means in dark ages, and among blind nations, the purpose is effected of preserving conscience and the belief of our immortality, without which the life of our life would be extinct? And with regard to the conjurers of the African and American savages, would it be unreasonable to suppose that, as the most elevated devotion brings us into fellowship with the Holy Spirit, a correspondent degree of wickedness may effect a communion with evil intelligences? These are mere speculations which I advance for as little as they are worth. My serious belief amounts to this, that preternatural impressions are sometimes communicated to us for wise purposes: and that departed spirits are sometimes permitted to manifest themselves.

Stranger.—If a ghost, then, were disposed to pay you a visit, you would be in a proper state of mind for receiving such a visitor?

Montesinos.—I should not credit my senses lightly; neither should I obstinately distrust them, after I had put the reality of the appearance to the proof, as far as that were possible.

Stranger.—Should you like to have an opportunity afforded you?

Montesinos.—Heaven forbid! I have suffered so much in dreams from conversing with those whom even in sleep I knew to be departed, that an actual presence might perhaps be more than I could bear.

Stranger.—But if it were the spirit of one with whom you had no near ties of relationship or love, how then would it affect you?

Montesinos.—That would of course be according to the circumstances on both sides. But I entreat you not to imagine that I am any way desirous of enduring the experiment.

Stranger.—Suppose, for example, he were to present himself as I have done; the purport of his coming friendly; the place and opportunity suiting, as at present; the time also considerately chosen—after dinner; and the spirit not more abrupt in his appearance nor more formidable in aspect than the being who now addresses you?

Montesinos.—Why, sir, to so substantial a ghost, and of such respectable appearance, I might, perhaps, have courage enough to say with Hamlet,

"Thou com'st in such a questionable shape,
That I will speak to thee!"

Stranger.—Then, sir, let me introduce myself in that character, now that our conversation has conducted us so happily to the point. I told you truly that I was English by birth, but that I came from a more distant country than America, and had long been naturalised there. The country whence I come is not the New World, but the other one: and I now declare myself in sober earnest to be a ghost.

Montesinos.—A ghost!

Stranger.—A veritable ghost, and an honest one, who went out of the world with so good a character that he will hardly escape canonisation if ever you get a Roman Catholic king upon the throne. And now what test do you require?

Montesinos.—I can detect no smell of brimstone; and the candle burns as it did before, without the slightest tinge of blue in its flame. You look, indeed, like a spirit of health, and I might be disposed to give entire belief to that countenance, if it were not for the tongue that belongs to it. But you are a queer spirit, whether good or evil!

Stranger.—The headsman thought so, when he made a ghost of me almost three hundred years ago. I had a character through life of loving a jest, and did not belie it at the last. But I had also as general a reputation for sincerity, and of that also conclusive proof was given at the same time. In serious truth, then, I am a disembodied spirit, and the form in which I now manifest myself is subject to none of the accidents of matter. You are still incredulous! Feel, then, and be convinced!

My incomprehensible guest extended his hand toward me as he spoke. I held forth mine to accept it, not, indeed, believing him, and yet not altogether without some apprehensive emotion, as if I were about to receive an electrical shock. The effect was more startling than electricity would have produced. His hand had neither weight nor substance; my fingers, when they would have closed upon it, found nothing that they could grasp: it was intangible, though it had all the reality of form.

"In the name of God," I exclaimed, "who are you, and wherefore are you come?"

"Be not alarmed," he replied. "Your reason, which has shown you the possibility of such an appearance as you now witness, must have convinced you also that it would never be permitted for an evil end. Examine my features well, and see if you do not recognise them. Hans Holbein was excellent at a likeness."

I had now for the first time in my life a distinct sense of that sort of porcupinish motion over the whole scalp which is so frequently described by the Latin poets. It was considerably allayed by the benignity of his countenance and the manner of his speech, and after looking him steadily in the face I ventured to say, for the likeness had previously struck me, "Is it Sir Thomas More?"

"The same," he made answer, and lifting up his chin, displayed a circle round the neck brighter in colour than the ruby. "The marks of martyrdom," he continued, "are our insignia of honour. Fisher and I have the purple collar, as Friar Forrest and Cranmer have the robe of fire."

A mingled feeling of fear and veneration kept me silent, till I perceived by his look that he expected and encouraged me to speak; and collecting my spirits as well as I could, I asked him wherefore he had thought proper to appear, and why to me rather than to any other person?

He replied, "We reap as we have sown. Men bear with them from this world into the intermediate state their habits of mind and stores of knowledge, their dispositions and affections and desires; and these become a part of our punishment, or of our reward, according to their kind. Those persons, therefore, in whom the virtue of patriotism has predominated continue to regard with interest their native land, unless it be so utterly sunk in degradation that the moral relationship between them is dissolved. Epaminondas can have no sympathy at this time with Thebes, nor Cicero with Rome, nor Belisarius with the imperial city of the East. But the worthies of England retain their affection for their noble country, behold its advancement with joy, and when serious danger appears to threaten the goodly structure of its institutions they feel as much anxiety as is compatible with their state of beatitude.

Montesinos.—What, then, may doubt and anxiety consist with the happiness of heaven?

Sir Thomas More.—Heaven and hell may be said to begin on your side the grave. In the intermediate state conscience anticipates with unerring certainty the result of judgment. We, therefore, who have done well can have no fear for ourselves. But inasmuch as the world has any hold upon our affections we are liable to that anxiety which is inseparable from terrestrial hopes. And as parents who are in bliss regard still with parental love the children whom they have left on earth, we, in like manner, though with a feeling different in kind and inferior in degree, look with apprehension upon the perils of our country.

"sub pectore forti
Vivit adhuc patriae pietas; stimulatque sepultum
Libertatis amor: pondus mortale necari
Si potuit, veteres animo post funera vires
Mansere, et prisci vivit non immemor aevi."

They are the words of old Mantuan.

Montesinos.—I am to understand, then, that you cannot see into the ways of futurity?

Sir Thomas More.—Enlarged as our faculties are, you must not suppose that we partake of prescience. For human actions are free, and we exist in time. The future is to us therefore as uncertain as to you; except only that having a clearer and more comprehensive knowledge of the past, we are enabled to reason better from causes to consequences, and by what has been to judge of what is likely to be. We have this advantage also, that we are divested of all those passions which cloud the intellects and warp the understandings of men. You are thinking, I perceive, how much you have to learn, and what you should first inquire of me. But expect no revelations! Enough was revealed when man was assured of judgment after death, and the means of salvation were afforded him. I neither come to discover secret things nor hidden treasures; but to discourse with you concerning these portentous and monster-breeding times; for it is your lot, as it was mine, to live during one of the grand climacterics of the world. And I come to you, rather than to any other person, because you have been led to meditate upon the corresponding changes whereby your age and mine are distinguished; and because, notwithstanding many discrepancies and some dispathies between us (speaking of myself as I was, and as you know me), there are certain points of sympathy and resemblance which bring us into contact, and enable us at once to understand each other.

Montesinos.—Et in Utopia ego.

Sir Thomas More.—You apprehend me. We have both speculated in the joys and freedom of our youth upon the possible improvement of society; and both in like manner have lived to dread with reason the effects of that restless spirit which, like the Titaness Mutability described by your immortal master, insults heaven and disturbs the earth. By comparing the great operating causes in the age of the Reformation, and in this age of revolutions, going back to the former age, looking at things as I then beheld them, perceiving wherein I judged rightly, and wherein I erred, and tracing the progress of those causes which are now developing their whole tremendous power, you will derive instruction, which you are a fit person to receive and communicate; for without being solicitous concerning present effect, you are contented to cast your bread upon the waters. You are now acquainted with me and my intention. To- morrow you will see me again; and I shall continue to visit you occasionally as opportunity may serve. Meantime say nothing of what has passed—not even to your wife. She might not like the thoughts of a ghostly visitor: and the reputation of conversing with the dead might be almost as inconvenient as that of dealing with the devil. For the present, then, farewell! I will never startle you with too sudden an apparition; but you may learn to behold my disappearance without alarm.

I was not able to behold it without emotion, although he had thus prepared me; for the sentence was no sooner completed than he was gone. Instead of rising from the chair he vanished from it. I know not to what the instantaneous disappearance can be likened. Not to the dissolution of a rainbow, because the colours of the rainbow fade gradually till they are lost; not to the flash of cannon, or to lightning, for these things are gone as so on as they are come, and it is known that the instant of their appearance must be that of their departure; not to a bubble upon the water, for you see it burst; not to the sudden extinction of a light, for that is either succeeded by darkness or leaves a different hue upon the surrounding objects. In the same indivisible point of time when I beheld the distinct, individual, and, to all sense of sight, substantial form— the living, moving, reasonable image—in that self-same instant it was gone, as if exemplifying the difference between to BE and NOT to BE. It was no dream, of this I was well assured; realities are never mistaken for dreams, though dreams may be mistaken for realities. Moreover I had long been accustomed in sleep to question my perceptions with a wakeful faculty of reason, and to detect their fallacy. But, as well may be supposed, my thoughts that night, sleeping as well as waking, were filled with this extraordinary interview; and when I arose the next morning it was not till I had called to mind every circumstance of time and place that I was convinced the apparition was real, and that I might again expect it.

COLLOQUY II

THE DEVELOPMENT OF THE WORLD

ON the following evening when my spiritual visitor entered the room, that volume of Dr. Wordsworth's ecclesiastical biography which contains his life was lying on the table beside me. "I perceive," said he, glancing at the book, "you have been gathering all you can concerning me from my good gossiping chronicler, who tells you that I loved milk and fruit and eggs, preferred beef to young meats, and brown bread to white; was fond of seeing strange birds and beasts, and kept an ape, a fox, a weasel, and a ferret."

"I am not one of those fastidious readers," I replied, "who quarrel with a writer for telling them too much. But these things were worth telling: they show that you retained a youthful palate as well as a youthful heart; and I like you the better both for your diet and your menagerie. The old biographer, indeed, with the best intentions, has been far from understanding the character which he desired to honour. He seems, however, to have been a faithful reporter, and has done as well as his capacity permitted. I observe that he gives you credit for 'a deep foresight and judgment of the times,' and for speaking in a prophetic spirit of the evils, which soon afterwards were 'full heavily felt.'"

"There could be little need for a spirit of prophecy," Sir Thomas made answer, to "foresee troubles which were the sure effect of the causes then in operation, and which were actually close at hand. When the rain is gathering from the south or west, and those flowers and herbs which serve as natural hygrometers close their leaves, men have no occasion to consult the stars for what the clouds and the earth are telling them. You were thinking of Prince Arthur when I introduced myself yesterday, as if musing upon the great events which seem to have received their bias from the apparent accident of his premature death."

Montesinos.—I had fallen into one of those idle reveries in which we speculate upon what might have been. Lord Bacon describes him as "very studious, and learned beyond his years, and beyond the custom of great princes." As this indicates a calm and thoughtful mind, it seems to show that he inherited the Tudor character. His brother took after the Plantagenets; but it was not of their nobler qualities that he partook. He had the popular manners of his grandfather, Edward IV., and, like him, was lustful, cruel, and unfeeling.

Sir Thomas More.—The blood of the Plantagenets, as your friends the Spaniards would say, was a strong blood. That temper of mind which (in some of his predecessors) thought so little of fratricide might perhaps have involved him in the guilt of a parricidal war, if his father had not been fortunate enough to escape such an affliction by a timely death. We might otherwise be allowed to wish that the life of Henry VII. had been prolonged to a good old age. For if ever there was a prince who could so have directed the Reformation as to have averted the evils wherewith that tremendous event was accompanied, and yet to have secured its advantages, he was the man. Cool, wary, far-sighted, rapacious, politic, and religious, or superstitious if you will (for his religion had its root rather in fear than in hope), he was peculiarly adapted for such a crisis both by his good and evil qualities. For the sake of increasing his treasures and his power, he would have promoted the Reformation; but his cautious temper, his sagacity, and his fear of Divine justice would have taught him where to stop.

Montesinos.—A generation of politic sovereigns succeeded to the race of warlike ones, just in that age of society when policy became of more importance in their station than military talents. Ferdinand of Spain, Joam II. whom the Portuguese called the perfect prince, Louis XI. and Henry VII. were all of this class. Their individual characters were sufficiently distinct; but the circumstances of their situation stamped them with a marked resemblance, and they were of a metal to take and retain the strong, sharp impress of the age.

Sir Thomas More.—The age required such characters; and it is worthy of notice how surely in the order of providence such men as are wanted are raised up. One generation of these princes sufficed. In Spain, indeed, there was an exception; for Ferdinand had two successors who pursued the same course of conduct. In the other kingdoms the character ceased with the necessity for it. Crimes enough were committed by succeeding sovereigns, but they were no longer the acts of systematic and reflecting policy. This, too, is worthy of remark, that the sovereigns whom you have named, and who scrupled at no means for securing themselves on the throne, for enlarging their dominions and consolidating their power, were each severally made to feel the vanity of human ambition, being punished either in or by the children who were to reap the advantage of their crimes. "Verily there is a God that judgeth the earth!"

Montesinos.—An excellent friend of mine, one of the wisest, best, and happiest men whom I have ever known, delights in this manner to trace the moral order of Providence through the revolutions of the world; and in his historical writings keeps it in view as the pole-star of his course. I wish he were present, that he might have the satisfaction of hearing his favourite opinion confirmed by one from the dead.

Sir Thomas More.—His opinion requires no other confirmation than what he finds for it in observation and Scripture, and in his own calm judgment. I should differ little from that friend of yours concerning the past; but his hopes for the future appear to me like early buds which are in danger of March winds. He believes the world to be in a rapid state of sure improvement; and in the ferment which exists everywhere he beholds only a purifying process; not considering that there is an acetous as well as a vinous fermentation; and that in the one case the liquor may be spilt, in the other it must be spoilt.

Montesinos.—Surely you would not rob us of our hopes for the human race! If I apprehended that your discourse tended to this end I should suspect you, notwithstanding your appearance, and be ready to exclaim, "Avaunt, tempter!" For there is no opinion from which I should so hardly be driven, and so reluctantly part, as the belief that the world will continue to improve, even as it has hitherto continually been improving; and that the progress of knowledge and the diffusion of Christianity will bring about at last, when men become

Christians in reality as well as in name, something like that Utopian state of which philosophers have loved to dream—like that millennium in which saints as well as enthusiasts have trusted.

Sir Thomas More.—Do you hold that this consummation must of necessity come to pass; or that it depends in any degree upon the course of events—that is to say, upon human actions? The former of these propositions you would be as unwilling to admit as your friend Wesley, or the old Welshman Pelagius himself. The latter leaves you little other foundation for your opinion than a desire, which, from its very benevolence, is the more likely to be delusive. You are in a dilemma.

Montesinos.—Not so, Sir Thomas. Impossible as it may be for us to reconcile the free will of man with the foreknowledge of God, I nevertheless believe in both with the most full conviction. When the human mind plunges into time and space in its speculations, it adventures beyond its sphere; no wonder, therefore, that its powers fail, and it is lost. But that my will is free, I know feelingly: it is proved to me by my conscience. And that God provideth all things I know by His own Word, and by that instinct which He hath implanted in me to assure me of His being. My answer to your question, then, is this: I believe that the happy consummation which I desire is appointed, and must come to pass; but that when it is to come depends upon the obedience of man to the will of God, that is, upon human actions.

Sir Thomas More.—You hold then that the human race will one day attain the utmost degree of general virtue, and thereby general happiness, of which humanity is capable. Upon what do you found this belief?

Montesinos.—The opinion is stated more broadly than I should choose to advance it. But this is ever the manner of argumentative discourse: the opponent endeavours to draw from you conclusions which you are not prepared to defend, and which perhaps you have never before acknowledged even to yourself. I will put the proposition in a less disputable form. A happier condition of society is possible than that in which any nation is existing at this time, or has at any time existed. The sum both of moral and physical evil may be greatly diminished both by good laws, good institutions, and good governments. Moral evil cannot indeed be removed, unless the nature of man were changed; and that renovation is only to be effected in individuals, and in them only by the special grace of God. Physical evil must always, to a certain degree, be inseparable from mortality. But both are so much within the reach of human institutions that a state of society is conceivable almost as superior to that of England in these days, as that itself is superior to the condition of the tattooed Britons, or of the northern pirates from whom we are descended. Surely this belief rests upon a reasonable foundation, and is supported by that general improvement (always going on if it be regarded upon the great scale) to which all history bears witness.

Sir Thomas More.—I dispute not this: but to render it a reasonable ground of immediate hope, the predominance of good principles must be supposed. Do you believe that good or evil principles predominate at this time?

Montesinos.—If I were to judge by that expression of popular opinion which the press pretends to convey, I should reply without hesitation that never in any other known age of the world have such pernicious principles been so prevalent

"Qua terra patet, fera regnat Erinnys;
In facinus jurasse putes."

Sir Thomas More.—Is there not a danger that these principles may bear down everything before them? and is not that danger obvious, palpable, imminent? Is there a considerate man who can look at the signs of the times without apprehension, or a scoundrel connected with what is called the public press, who does not speculate upon them, and join with the anarchists as the strongest party? Deceive not yourself by the fallacious notion that truth is mightier than falsehood, and that good must prevail over evil! Good principles enable men to suffer, rather than to act. Think how the dog, fond and faithful creature as he is, from being the most docile and obedient of all animals, is made the most dangerous, if he becomes mad; so men acquire a frightful and not less monstrous power when they are in a state of moral insanity, and break loose from their social and religious obligations. Remember too how rapidly the plague of diseased opinions is communicated, and that if it once gain head, it is as difficult to be stopped as a conflagration or a flood. The prevailing opinions of this age go to the destruction of everything which has hitherto been held sacred. They tend to arm the poor against the rich; the many against the few: worse than this, for it will also be a war of hope and enterprise against timidity, of youth against age.

Montesinos.—Sir Ghost, you are almost as dreadful an alarmist as our Cumberland cow, who is believed to have lately uttered this prophecy, delivering it with oracular propriety in verse:

"Two winters, a wet spring,
A bloody summer, and no king."

Sir Thomas More.—That prophecy speaks the wishes of the man, whoever he may have been, by whom it was invented: and you who talk of the progress of knowledge, and the improvement of society, and upon that improvement build your hope of its progressive melioration, you know that even so gross and palpable an imposture as this is swallowed by many of the vulgar, and contributes in its sphere to the mischief which it was designed to promote. I admit that such an improved condition of society as you contemplate is possible, and hath ought always to be kept in view: but the error of supposing it too near, of fancying that there is a short road to it, is, of all the errors of these times, the most pernicious, because it seduces the young and generous, and betrays them imperceptibly into an alliance with whatever is flagitious and detestable. The fact is undeniable that the worst principles in religion, in morals, and in politics, are at this time more prevalent than they ever were known to be in any former age. You need not be told in what manner revolutions in opinion bring about the fate of empires; and upon this ground you ought to regard the state of the world, both at home and abroad, with fear, rather than with hope.

Montesinos.—When I have followed such speculations as may allowably be indulged, respecting what is hidden in the darkness of time and of eternity, I have sometimes thought that the moral and physical order of the world may be so appointed as to coincide; and that the revolutions of this planet may correspond with the condition of its inhabitants; so that the convulsions and changes whereto it is destined should occur, when the existing race of men had either become so corrupt as to be unworthy of the place which they hold in the universe, or were so truly regenerate by the will and word of God, as to be qualified for a higher station in it. Our globe may have gone through many such revolutions. We know the history of the last; the measure of its wickedness was then filled up. For the future we are taught to expect a happier consummation.

Sir Thomas More.—It is important that you should distinctly understand the nature and extent of your expectations on that head. Is it upon the Apocalypse that you rest them?

Montesinos.—If you had not forbidden me to expect from this intercourse any communication which might come with the authority of revealed knowledge, I should ask in reply, whether that dark book is indeed to be received for authentic Scripture? My hopes are derived from the prophets and the evangelists. Believing in them with a calm and settled faith, with that consent of the will and heart and understanding which constitutes religious belief, and in them the clear annunciation of that kingdom of God upon earth, for the coming of which Christ himself has taught and commanded us to pray.

Sir Thomas More.—Remember that the Evangelists, in predicting that kingdom, announce a dreadful advent! And that, according to the received opinion of the Church, wars, persecutions, and calamities of every kind, the triumph of evil, and the coming of Antichrist are to be looked for, before the promises made by the prophets shall be fulfilled. Consider this also, that the speedy fulfilment of those promises has been the ruling fancy of the most dangerous of all madmen, from John of Leyden and his frantic followers, down to the saints of Cromwell's army, Venner and his Fifth-Monarchy men, the fanatics of the Cevennes, and the blockheads of your own days, who beheld with complacency the crimes of the French Revolutionists, and the progress of Bonaparte towards the subjugation of Europe, as events tending to bring about the prophecies; and, under the same besotted persuasion, are ready at this time to co-operate with the miscreants who trade in blasphemy and treason! But you who neither seek to deceive others nor yourself, you who are neither insane nor insincere, you surely do not expect that the millennium is to be brought about by the triumph of what are called liberal opinions; nor by enabling the whole of the lower classes to read the incentives to vice, impiety, and rebellion which are prepared for them by an unlicensed press; nor by Sunday schools, and religious tract societies; nor by the portentous bibliolatry of the age! And if you adhere to the letter of the Scriptures, methinks the thought of that consummation for which you look, might serve rather for consolation under the prospect of impending evils, than for a hope upon which the mind can rest in security with a calm and contented delight.

Montesinos.—To this I must reply, that the fulfilment of those calamitous events predicted in the Gospels may safely be referred, as it usually is, and by the best Biblical scholars, to the destruction of Jerusalem. Concerning the visions of the Apocalypse, sublime as they are, I speak with less hesitation, and dismiss them from my thoughts, as more congenial to the fanatics of whom you have spoken than to me. And for the coming of Antichrist, it is no longer a received opinion in these days, whatever it may have been in yours. Your reasoning applies to the enthusiastic millenarians who discover the number of the beast, and calculate the year when a vial is to be poured out, with as much precision as the day and hour of an eclipse. But it leaves my hope unshaken and untouched. I know that the world has improved; I see that it is improving; and I believe that it will continue to improve in natural and certain progress. Good and evil principles are widely at work: a crisis is evidently approaching; it may be dreadful, but I can have no doubts concerning the result. Black and ominous as the aspects may appear, I regard them without dismay. The common exclamation of the poor and helpless, when they feel themselves oppressed, conveys to my mind the sum of the surest and safest philosophy. I say with them, "God is above," and trust Him for the event.

Sir Thomas More.—God is above—but the devil is below. Evil principles are, in their nature, more active than good. The harvest is precarious, and must be prepared with labour, and cost, and care; weeds spring up of themselves, and flourish and seed whatever may be the season. Disease, vice, folly, and madness are contagious; while health and understanding are incommunicable, and wisdom and virtue hardly to be communicated! We have come, however, to some conclusion in our discourse. Your notion of the improvement of the world has appeared to be a mere speculation, altogether inapplicable in practice; and as dangerous to weak heads and heated imaginations as it is congenial to benevolent hearts. Perhaps that improvement is neither so general nor so certain as you suppose. Perhaps, even in this country there may be more knowledge than there was in former times and less wisdom, more wealth and less happiness, more display and less virtue. This must be the subject of future conversation. I will only remind you now, that the French had persuaded themselves this was the most enlightened age of the world, and they the most enlightened people in it—the politest, the most amiable, and the most humane of nations—and that a new era of philosophy, philanthropy, and peace, was about to commence under their auspices, when they were upon the eve of a revolution which, for its complicated monstrosities, absurdities, and horrors, is more disgraceful to human nature than any other series of events in history. Chew the cud upon this, and farewell

COLLOQUY III

THE DRUIDICAL STONES
VISITATIONS OF PESTILENCE

INCLINATION would lead me to hibernate during half the year in this uncomfortable climate of Great Britain, where few men who have tasted the enjoyments of a better would willingly take up their abode, if it were not for the habits, and still more for the ties and duties which root us to our native soil. I envy the Turks for their sedentary constitutions, which seem no more to require exercise than an oyster does or a toad in a stone. In this respect, I am by disposition as true a Turk as the Grand Seignior himself; and approach much nearer to one in the habit of inaction than any person of my acquaintance. Willing however, as I should be to believe, that anything which is habitually necessary for a sound body, would be unerringly indicated by an habitual disposition for it, and that if exercise were as needful as food for the preservation of the animal economy, the desire of motion would recur not less regularly than hunger and thirst, it is a theory which will not bear the test; and this I know by experience.

On a grey sober day, therefore, and in a tone of mind quite accordant with the season, I went out unwillingly to take the air, though if taking physic would have answered the same purpose, the dose would have been preferred as the shortest, and for that reason the least unpleasant remedy. Even on such occasions as this, it is desirable to propose to oneself some object for the satisfaction of accomplishing it, and to set out with the intention of reaching some fixed point, though it should be nothing better than a mile-stone, or a directing post. So I walked to the Circle of Stones on the Penrith road, because there is a long hill upon the way which would give the muscles some work to perform; and because the sight of this rude monument which has stood during so many centuries, and is likely, if left to itself, to outlast any edifice that man could have erected, gives me always a feeling, which, however often it may be repeated, loses nothing of its force.

The circle is of the rudest kind, consisting of single stones, unhewn and chosen without any regard to shape or magnitude, being of all sizes, from seven or eight feet in height, to three or four. The circle, however, is complete, and is thirty-three paces in diameter. Concerning this, like all similar monuments in Great Britain, the popular superstition prevails, that no two persons can number the stones alike, and that no person will ever find a second counting confirm the first. My children have often disappointed their natural inclination to believe this wonder, by putting it to the test and disproving it. The number of the stones which compose the circle, is thirty-eight, and besides these there are ten which form three sides of a little square within, on the eastern side, three stones of the circle itself forming the fourth; this being evidently the place where the Druids who presided had their station; or where the more sacred and important part of the rites and ceremonies (whatever they may have been) were performed. All this is as perfect at this day as when the Cambrian bards, according to the custom of their ancient order, described by my old acquaintances, the living members of the Chair of Glamorgan, met there for the last time,

"On the green turf and under the blue sky,
Their heads in reverence bare, and bare of foot."

The site also precisely accords with the description which Edward Williams and William Owen give of the situation required for such meeting places:

"—a high hill top,
Nor bowered with trees, nor broken by the plough:
Remote from human dwellings and the stir
Of human life, and open to the breath
And to the eye of Heaven."

The high hill is now enclosed and cultivated; and a clump of larches has been planted within the circle, for the purpose of protecting an oak in the centre, the owner of the field having wished to rear one there with a commendable feeling, because that tree was held sacred by the Druids, and therefore, he supposed, might be appropriately placed there. The whole plantation, however, has been so miserably storm-stricken that the poor stunted trees are not even worth the trouble of cutting them down for fuel, and so they continue to disfigure the spot. In all other respects this impressive monument of former times is carefully preserved; the soil within the enclosure is not broken, a path from the road is left, and in latter times a stepping-stile has been placed to accommodate Lakers with an easier access than by striding over the gate beside it.

The spot itself is the most commanding which could be chosen in this part of the country, without climbing a mountain. Derwentwater and the Vale of Keswick are not seen from it, only the mountains which enclose them on the south and west. Lattrigg and the huge side of Skiddaw are on the north; to the east is the open country towards Penrith expanding from the Vale of St. John's, and extending for many miles, with Mellfell in the distance, where it rises alone like a huge tumulus on the right, and Blencathra on the left, rent into deep ravines. On the south-east is the range of Helvellyn, from its termination at Wanthwaite Crags to its loftiest summits, and to Dunmailraise. The lower range of Nathdalefells lies nearer, in a parallel line with Helvellyn; and the dale itself, with its little streamlet, immediately below. The heights above Leatheswater, with the Borrowdale mountains, complete the panorama.

While I was musing upon the days of the Bards and Druids, and thinking that Llywarc Hen himself had probably stood within this very circle at a time when its history was known, and the rites for which it was erected still in use, I saw a person approaching, and started a little at perceiving that it was my new acquaintance from the world of spirits. "I am come," said he, "to join company with you in your walk: you may as well converse with a ghost as stand dreaming of the dead. I dare say you have been wishing that these stones could speak and tell their tale, or that some record were sculptured upon them, though it were as unintelligible as the hieroglyphics, or as an Ogham inscription."

"My ghostly friend," I replied, "they tell me something to the purport of our last discourse. Here upon ground where the Druids have certainly held their assemblies, and where not improbably, human sacrifices have been offered up, you will find it difficult to maintain that the improvement of the world has not been unequivocal, and very great."

Sir Thomas More.—Make the most of your vantage ground! My position is, that this improvement is not general; that while some parts of the earth are progressive in civilisation, others have been retrograde; and that even where improvement appears the greatest, it is partial. For example; with all the meliorations which have taken place in England since these stones were set up (and you will not suppose that I who laid down my life for a religious principle, would undervalue the most important of all advantages), do you believe that they have extended to all classes? Look at the question well. Consider your fellow-countrymen, both in their physical and intellectual relations, and tell me whether a large portion of the community are in a happier or more hopeful condition at this time, than their forefathers were when Caesar set foot upon the island?

Montesinos.—If it be your aim to prove that the savage state is preferable to the social, I am perhaps the very last person upon whom any arguments to that end could produce the slightest effect. That notion never for a moment deluded me: not even in the ignorance and presumptuousness of youth, when first I perused Rousseau, and was unwilling to feel that a writer whose passionate eloquence I felt and admired so truly could be erroneous in any of his opinions. But now, in the evening of life, when I know upon what foundation my principles rest, and when the direction of one peculiar course of study has made it necessary for me to learn everything which books could teach concerning savage life, the proposition appears to me one of the most untenable that ever was advanced by a perverse or a paradoxical intellect.

Sir Thomas More.—I advanced no such paradox, and you have answered me too hastily. The Britons were not savages when the Romans invaded and improved them. They were already far advanced in the barbarous stage of society, having the use of metals, domestic cattle, wheeled carriages, and money, a settled government, and a regular priesthood, who were connected with their fellow-Druids on the Continent, and who were not ignorant of letters. Understand me! I admit that improvements of the utmost value have been made, in the most important concerns: but I deny that the melioration has been general; and insist, on the contrary, that a considerable portion of the people are in a state, which, as relates to their physical condition, is greatly worsened, and, as touching their intellectual nature, is assuredly not improved. Look, for example, at the great mass of your populace in town and country—a tremendous proportion of the whole community! Are their bodily wants better, or more easily supplied? Are they subject to fewer calamities? Are they happier in childhood, youth, and manhood, and more comfortably or carefully provided for in old age, than when the land was unenclosed, and half covered with woods? With regard to their moral and intellectual capacity, you well know how little of the light of knowledge and of revelation has reached them. They are still in darkness, and in the shadow of death!

Montesinos.—I perceive your drift: and perceive also that when we understand each other there is likely to be little difference between us. And I beseech you, do not suppose that I am disputing for the sake of disputation; with that pernicious habit I was never infected, and I have seen too many mournful proofs of its perilous consequences. Towards any person it is injudicious and offensive; towards you it would be irreverent. Your position is undeniable. Were society to be stationary at its present point, the bulk of the people would, on the whole, have lost rather than gained by the alterations which have taken place during the last thousand years. Yet this must be remembered, that in common with all ranks they are exempted from those dreadful visitations of war, pestilence, and famine by which these kingdoms were so frequently afflicted of old.

The countenance of my companion changed upon this, to an expression of judicial severity which struck me with awe. "Exempted from these visitations!" he exclaimed; "mortal man! creature of a day, what art thou, that thou shouldst presume upon any such exemption! Is it from a trust in your own deserts, or a reliance upon the forbearance and long-suffering of the Almighty, that this vain confidence arises?"

I was silent.

"My friend," he resumed, in a milder tone, but with a melancholy manner, "your own individual health and happiness are scarcely more precarious than this fancied security. By the mercy of God, twice during the short space of your life, England has been spared from the horrors of invasion, which might with ease have been effected during the American war, when the enemy's fleet swept the Channel, and insulted your very ports, and which was more than once seriously intended during the late long contest. The invaders would indeed have found their graves in that soil which they came to subdue: but before they could have been overcome, the atrocious threat of Buonaparte's general might have been in great part realised, that though he could not answer for effecting the conquest of England, he would engage to destroy its prosperity for a century to come. You have been spared from that chastisement. You have escaped also from the imminent danger of peace with a military tyrant, which would inevitably have led to invasion, when he should have been ready to undertake and accomplish that great object of his ambition, and you must have been least prepared and least able to resist him. But if the seeds of civil war should at this time be quickening among you— if your soil is everywhere sown with the dragon's teeth, and the fatal crop be at this hour ready to spring up—the impending evil will be a hundredfold more terrible than those which have been averted; and you will have cause to perceive and acknowledge, that the wrath has been suspended only that it may fall the heavier!"

"May God avert this also!" I exclaimed.

"As for famine," he pursued, "that curse will always follow in the train of war: and even now the public tranquillity of England is fearfully dependent upon the seasons. And touching pestilence, you fancy yourselves secure, because the plague has not appeared among you for the last hundred and fifty years: a portion of time, which long as it may seem when compared with the brief term of mortal existence, is as nothing in the physical history of the globe. The importation of that scourge is as possible now as it was in former times: and were it once imported, do you suppose it would rage with less violence among the crowded population of your metropolis, than it did before the fire, or that it would not reach parts of the country which were never infected in any former visitation? On the contrary, its ravages would be more general and more tremendous, for it would inevitably be carried everywhere. Your provincial cities have doubled and trebled in size; and in London itself, great part of the population is as much crowded now as it was then, and the space which is covered with houses is increased at least fourfold. What if the sweating-sickness, emphatically called the English disease, were to show itself again? Can any cause be assigned why it is not as likely to break out in the nineteenth century as in the fifteenth? What if your manufactures, according to the ominous opinion which your greatest physiologist has expressed, were to generate for you new physical plagues, as they have already produced a moral pestilence unknown to all preceding ages? What if the small-pox, which you vainly believed to be subdued, should have assumed a new and more formidable character; and (as there seems no trifling grounds for apprehending) instead of being protected by vaccination from its danger, you should ascertain that inoculation itself affords no certain security? Visitations of this kind are in the order of nature and of providence. Physically considered, the likelihood of their recurrence becomes every year more probable than the last; and looking to the moral government of the world, was there ever a time when the sins of this kingdom called more cryingly for chastisement?

Montesinos.—[Greek text which cannot be reproduced]

Sir Thomas More.—I denounce no judgments. But I am reminding you that there is as much cause for the prayer in your Litany against plague, pestilence, and famine, as for that which entreats God to deliver you all from sedition, privy conspiracy, and rebellion; from all false doctrine, heresy, and schism. In this, as in all things, it behoves the Christian to live in a humble and grateful sense of his continual dependence upon the Almighty: not to rest in a presumptuous confidence upon the improved state of human knowledge, or the altered course of natural visitations.

Montesinos.—Oh, how wholesome it is to receive instruction with a willing and a humble mind! In attending to your discourse I feel myself in the healthy state of a pupil, when without one hostile or contrarient prepossession, he listens to a teacher in whom he has entire confidence. And I feel also how much better it is that the authority of elder and wiser intellects should pass even for more than it is worth, than that it should be undervalued as in these days, and set at nought. When any person boasts that he is -

"Nullias addictus jurare in verba magistri,"

the reason of that boast may easily be perceived; it is because he thinks, like

Jupiter, that it would be disparaging his own all- wiseness to swear by anything but himself. But wisdom will as little enter into a proud or a conceited mind as into a malicious one. In this sense also it may be said, that he who humbleth himself shall be exalted.

Sir Thomas More.—It is not implicit assent that I require, but reasonable conviction after calm and sufficient consideration. David was permitted to choose between the three severest dispensations of God's displeasure, and he made choice of pestilence as the least dreadful. Ought a reflecting and religious man to be surprised, if some such punishment were dispensed to this country, not less in mercy than in judgment, as the means of averting a more terrible and abiding scourge? An endemic malady, as destructive as the plague, has naturalised itself among your American brethren, and in Spain. You have hitherto escaped it, speaking with reference to secondary causes, merely because it has not yet been imported. But any season may bring it to your own shores; or at any hour it may appear among you homebred.

Montesinos.—We should have little reason, then, to boast of our improvements in the science of medicine; for our practitioners at Gibraltar found themselves as unable to stop its progress, or mitigate its symptoms, as the most ignorant empirics in the peninsula.

Sir Thomas More.—You were at one time near enough that pestilence to feel as if you were within its reach?

Montesinos.—It was in 1800, the year when it first appeared in Andalusia. That summer I fell in at Cintra with a young German, on the way from his own country to his brothers at Cadiz, where they were established as merchants. Many days had not elapsed after his arrival in that city when a ship which was consigned to their firm brought with it the infection; and the first news which reached us of our poor acquaintance was that the yellow fever had broken out in his brother's house, and that he, they, and the greater part of the household, were dead. There was every reason to fear that the pestilence would extend into Portugal, both governments being, as usual, slow in providing any measures of precaution, and those measures being nugatory when taken. I was at Faro in the ensuing spring, at the house of Mr. Lempriere, the British Consul. Inquiring of him upon the subject, the old man lifted up his hands, and replied in a passionate manner, which I shall never forget, "Oh, sir, we escaped by the mercy of God; only by the mercy of God!" The governor of Algarve, even when the danger was known and acknowledged, would not venture to prohibit the communication with Spain till he received orders from Lisbon; and then the prohibition was so enforced as to be useless. The crew of a boat from the infected province were seized and marched through the country to Tavira: they were then sent to perform quarantine upon a little insulated ground, and the guards who were set over them, lived with them, and were regularly relieved. When such were the precautionary measures, well indeed might it be said, that Portugal escaped only by the mercy of God! I have often reflected upon the little effect which this imminent danger appeared to produce upon those persons with whom I associated. The young, with that hilarity which belongs to thoughtless youth, used to converse about the places whither they should retire, and the course of life and expedients to which they should be driven in case it were necessary for them to fly from Lisbon. A few elder and more considerate persons said little upon the subject, but that little denoted a deep sense of the danger, and more anxiety than they thought proper to express. The great majority seemed to be altogether unconcerned; neither their business nor their amusements were interrupted; they feasted, they danced, they met at the card-table as usual; and the plague (for so it was called at that time, before its nature was clearly understood) was as regular a topic of conversation as the news brought by the last packet.

Sir Thomas More.—And what was your own state of mind?

Montesinos.—Very much what it has long been with regard to the moral pestilence of this unhappy age, and the condition of this country more especially. I saw the danger in its whole extent and relied on the mercy of God.

Sir Thomas More.—In all cases that is the surest reliance: but when human means are available, it becomes a Mahommedan rather than a Christian to rely upon Providence or fate alone, and make no effort for its own preservation. Individuals never fall into this error among you, drink as deeply as they may of fatalism; that narcotic will sometimes paralyse the moral sense, but it leaves the faculty of worldly prudence unimpaired. Far otherwise is it with your government: for such are the notions of liberty in England, that evils of every kind—physical, moral, and political, are allowed their free range. As relates to infectious diseases, for example, this kingdom is now in a less civilised state than it was in my days, three centuries ago, when the leper was separated from general society; and when, although the science of medicine was at once barbarous and fantastical, the existence of pesthouses showed at least some approaches towards a medical police.

Montesinos.—They order these things better in Utopia.

Sir Thomas More.—In this, as well as in some other points upon which we shall touch hereafter, the difference between you and the Utopians is as great as between the existing generation and the race by whom yonder circle was set up. With regard to diseases and remedies in general, the real state of the case may be consolatory, but it is not comfortable. Great and certain progress has been made in chirurgery; and if the improvements in the other branch of medical science have not been so certain and so great, it is because the physician works in the dark, and has to deal with what is hidden and mysterious. But the evils for which these sciences are the palliatives have increased in a proportion that heavily overweighs the benefit of improved therapeutics. For as the intercourse between nations has become greater, the evils of one have been communicated to another. Pigs, Spanish dollars, and Norway rats, are not the only commodities and incommodities which have performed the circumnavigation, and are to be found wherever European ships have touched. Diseases also find their way from one part of the inhabited globe to another, wherever it is possible for them to exist. The most formidable endemic or contagious maladies in your nosology are not indigenous; and as far as regards health therefore, the ancient Britons, with no other remedies than their fields and woods afforded them, and no other medical practitioners than their deceitful priests, were in a better condition than their descendants, with all the instruction which is derived from Sydenham and Heberden, and Hunter, and with all the powers which chemistry has put into their hands.

Montesinos.—You have well said that there is nothing comfortable in this view of the case: but what is there consolatory in it?

Sir Thomas More.—The consolation is upon your principle of expectant hope. Whenever improved morals, wiser habits, more practical religion, and more efficient institutions shall have diminished the moral and material causes of disease, a thoroughly scientific practice, the result of long experience and accumulated observations, will then exist, to remedy all that is within the power of human art, and to alleviate what is irremediable. To existing individuals this consolation is something like the satisfaction you might feel in learning that a fine estate was entailed upon your family at the expiration of a lease of ninety-nine years from the present time. But I had forgotten to whom I am talking. A poet always looks onward to some such distant inheritance. His hopes are usually in nubibus, and his expectations in the paulo post futurum tense.

Montesinos.—His state is the more gracious then because his enjoyment is always to come. It is however a real satisfaction to me that there is some sunshine in your prospect.

Sir Thomas More.—More in mine than in yours, because I command a wider horizon: but I see also the storms which are blackening, and may close over the sky. Our discourse began concerning that portion of the community who form the base of the pyramid; we have unawares taken a more general view, but it has not led us out of the way. Returning to the most numerous class of society, it is apparent that in the particular point of which we have been conversing, their condition is greatly worsened: they remain liable to the same indigenous diseases as their forefathers, and are exposed moreover to all which have been imported. Nor will the estimate of their condition be improved upon farther inquiry. They are worse fed than when they were hunters, fishers, and herdsmen; their clothing and habitations are little better, and, in comparison with those of the higher classes, immeasurably worse. Except in the immediate vicinity of the collieries, they suffer more from cold than when the woods and turbaries were open. They are less religious than in the days of the Romish faith; and if we consider them in relation to their immediate superiors, we shall find reason to confess that the independence which has been gained since the total decay of the feudal system, has been dearly purchased by the loss of kindly feelings and ennobling attachments. They are less contented, and in no respect more happy—that look implies hesitation of judgment, and an unwillingness to be convinced. Consider the point; go to your books and your thoughts; and when next we meet, you will feel little inclination to dispute the irrefragable statement.

COLLOQUY IV

FEUDAL SLAVERY
GROWTH OF PAUPERISM

THE last conversation had left a weight upon me, which was not lessened when I contemplated the question in solitude. I called to mind the melancholy view which Young has taken of the world in his unhappy poem:

"A part how small of the terraqueous globe
Is tenanted by man! the rest a waste,
Rocks, deserts, frozen seas and burning sands,
Wild haunts of monsters, poisons, stings, and death.
Such is earth's melancholy map! But, far
More sad, this earth is a true map of man."

Sad as this representation is, I could not but acknowledge that the moral and intellectual view is not more consolatory than the poet felt it to be; and it was a less sorrowful consideration to think how large a portion of the habitable earth is possessed by savages, or by nations whom inhuman despotisms and monstrous superstitions have degraded in some respects below the savage state, than to observe how small a part of what is called the civilised world is truly civilised; and in the most civilised parts to how small a portion of the inhabitants the real blessings of civilisation are confined. In this mood how heartily should I have accorded with Owen of Lanark if I could have agreed with that happiest and most beneficent and most practical of all enthusiasts as well concerning the remedy as the disease!

"Well, Montesinos," said the spirit, when he visited me next, "have you recollected or found any solid arguments for maintaining that the labouring classes, who form the great bulk of the population, are in a happier condition, physical, moral, or intellectual, in these times, than they were in mine?"

Montesinos.—Perhaps, Sir Thomas, their condition was better precisely during your age than it ever has been either before or since. The feudal system had well-nigh lost all its inhuman parts, and the worse inhumanity of the commercial system had not yet shown itself.

Sir Thomas More.—It was, indeed, a most important age in English history, and, till the Reformation so fearfully disturbed it, in many respects a happy and an enviable one. But the process was then beginning which is not yet completed. As the feudal system relaxed and tended to dissolution the condition of the multitude was changed. Let us trace it from earlier times! In what state do you suppose the people of this island to have been when they were invaded by the Romans?

Montesinos.—Something worse than the Greeks of the Homeric age: something better than the Sandwich or Tonga islanders when they were visited by Captain Cook. Inferior to the former in arts, in polity, and, above all, in their domestic institutions; superior to the latter as having the use of cattle and being under a superstition in which, amid many abominations, some patriarchal truths were preserved. Less fortunate in physical circumstances than either, because of the climate.

Sir Thomas More.—A viler state of morals than their polyandrian system must have produced can scarcely be imagined; and the ferocity of their manners, little as is otherwise known of them, is sufficiently shown by their scythed war-chariots, and the fact that in the open country the path from one town to another was by a covered way. But in what condition were the labouring classes?

Montesinos.—In slavery, I suppose. When the Romans first attacked the island it was believed at Rome that slaves were the only booty which Britain could afford; and slaves, no doubt, must have been the staple commodity for which its ports were visited. Different tribes had at different times established themselves here by conquest, and wherever settlements are thus made slavery is the natural consequence. It was a part of the Roman economy; and when the Saxons carved out their kingdoms with the sword, the slaves, and their masters too, if any survived, became the property of the new lords of the land, like the cattle who pastured upon it. It is not likely even that the Saxons should have brought artificers of any kind with them, smiths perhaps alone excepted. Trades of every description must have been practised by the slaves whom they found. The same sort of transfer ensued upon the Norman conquest. After that event there could have been no fresh supply of domestic slaves, unless they were imported from Ireland, as well as carried thither for sale. That trade did not continue long. Emancipation was promoted by the clergy, and slavery was exchanged for vassalage, which in like manner gradually disappeared as the condition of the people improved.

Sir Thomas More.—You are hurrying too fast to that conclusion. Hitherto more has been lost than gained in morals by the transition; and you will not maintain that anything which is morally injurious can be politically advantageous. Vassalage I know is a word which bears no favourable acceptation in this liberal age; and slavery is in worse repute. But we must remember that slavery implies a very different state in different ages of the world, and in different stages of society.

Montesinos.—In many parts of the East, and of the Mohammedan world, as in the patriarchal times, it is scarcely an evil. Among savages it is as little so. In a luxurious state more vices are called into action, the condition of the slave depends more upon the temper of the owner, and the evil then predominates. But slavery is nowhere so bad as in commercial colonies, where the desire of gain hardens the heart—the basest appetites have free scope there; and the worst passions are under little restraint from law, less from religion, and none from public opinion.

Sir Thomas More.—You have omitted in this enumeration that kind of slavery which existed in England.

Montesinos.—The slavery of the feudal ages may perhaps be classed midway between the best description of that state and the worst. I suppose it to have been less humane than it generally is in Turkey, less severe than it generally was in Rome and Greece. In too many respects the slaves were at the mercy of their lords. They might be put in irons and punished with stripes; they were sometimes branded; and there is proof that it has been the custom to yoke them in teams like cattle.

Sir Thomas More.—Are you, then, Montesinos, so much the dupe of words as to account among their grievances a mere practice of convenience?

Montesinos.—The reproof was merited. But I was about to say that there is no reason to think their treatment was generally rigorous. We do not hear of any such office among them as that of the Roman Lorarii, whose office appears by the dramatists to have been no sinecure. And it is certain that they possessed in the laws, in the religion, and probably in the manners of the country, a greater degree of protection than existed to alleviate the lot of the Grecian and Roman slaves.

Sir Thomas More.—The practical difference between the condition of the feudal slave, and of the labouring husbandman who succeeded to the business of his station, was mainly this, that the former had neither the feeling nor the insecurity of independence. He served one master as long as he lived; and being at all times sure of the same sufficient subsistence, if he belonged to the estate like the cattle, and was accounted with them as part of the live stock, he resembled them also in the exemption which he enjoyed from all cares concerning his own maintenance and that of his family. The feudal slaves, indeed, were subject to none of those vicissitudes which brought so many of the proudest and most powerful barons to a disastrous end. They had nothing to lose, and they had liberty to hope for; frequently as the reward of their own faithful services, and not seldom from the piety or kindness of their lords. This was a steady hope depending so little upon contingency that it excited no disquietude or restlessness. They were therefore in general satisfied with the lot to which they were born, as the Greenlander is with his climate, the Bedouin with his deserts, and the Hottentot and the Calmuck with their filthy and odious customs; and going on in their regular and unvaried course of duty generation after generation, they were content.

Montesinos.—"Fish, fish, are you in your duty?" said the young lady in the Arabian tales, who came out of the kitchen wall clad in flowered satin, and with a rod in her hand. The fish lifted up their heads and replied, "Yes, yes; if you reckon, we reckon; if you pay your debts we pay ours; if you fly we overcome, and are content." The fish who were thus content, and in their duty, had been gutted, and were in the frying-pan. I do not seek, however, to escape from the force of your argument by catching at the words. On the other hand, I am sure it is not your intention to represent slavery otherwise than as an evil, under any modification.

Sir Thomas More.—That which is a great evil in itself become relatively a good when it prevents or removes a greater evil; for instance, loss of a limb when life is preserved by the sacrifice, or the acute pain of a remedy by which a chronic disease is cured. Such was slavery in its origin: a commutation for death, gladly accepted as mercy under the arm of a conqueror in battle, or as the mitigation of a judicial sentence. But it led immediately to nefarious abuses; and the earliest records which tell us of its existence show us also that men were kidnapped for sale. With the principles of Christianity, the principles of religious philosophy— the only true policy, to which mankind must come at last, by which alone all the remediable ills of humanity are to be remedied, and for which you are taught to pray when you entreat that your Father's kingdom may come—with those principles slavery is inconsistent, and therefore not to be tolerated, even in speculation.

Montesinos.—Yet its fitness, as a commutation for other punishments, is admitted by Michaelis (though he decides against it) to be one of the most difficult questions connected with the existing state of society. And in the age of the Revolution, one of the sturdiest Scotch republicans proposed the reestablishment of slavery, as the best or only means for correcting the vices and removing the miseries of the poor.

Sir Thomas More.—The proposal of such a remedy must be admitted as full proof of the malignity of the disease. And in further excuse of Andrew Fletcher, it should be remembered that he belonged to a country where many of the feudal virtues (as well as most of the feudal vices) were at that time in full vigour. But let us return to our historical view of the subject. In feudal servitude there was no motive for cruelty, scarcely any for oppression. There were no needy slave-owners, as there are in commercial colonies; and though slaves might sometimes suffer from a wicked, or even a passionate master, there is no reason to believe that they were habitually over-tasked, or subjected to systematic ill-treatment; for that, indeed, can only arise from avarice, and avarice is not the vice of feudal times. Still, however, slavery is intolerable upon Christian principles; and to the influence of those principles it yielded here in England. It had ceased, so as even to be forgotten in my youth; and villenage was advancing fast towards its natural extinction. The courts decided that a tenant having a lease could not be a villein during its term, for if his labour were at the command of another how could he undertake to pay rent? Landholders had thus to choose between rent and villenage, and scarcely wanted the Field of the Cloth of Gold at Ardres to show them which they stood most in need of. And as villenage disappeared, free labourers of various descriptions multiplied; of whom the more industrious and fortunate rose in society, and became tradesmen and merchants; the unlucky and the reprobate became vagabonds.

Montesinos.—The latter class appears to have been far more numerous in your age than in mine.

Sir Thomas More.—Waiving for the present the question whether they really were so, they appear to have been so partly in consequence of the desperate wars between the houses of York and Lancaster, partly because of the great change in society which succeeded to that contest. During those wars both parties exerted themselves to bring into the field all the force they could muster. Villeins in great numbers were then emancipated, when they were embodied in arms; and great numbers emancipated themselves, flying to London and other cities for protection from the immediate evils of war, or taking advantage of the frequent changes of property, and the precarious tenure by which it was held, to exchange their own servile condition for a station of freedom with all its hopes and chances. This took place to a great extent, and the probabilities of success were greatly in their favour; for whatever may have been practised in earlier and ruder times, in that age they certainly were not branded like cattle, according to the usage of your sugar islands.

Montesinos.—A planter, who notwithstanding this curious specimen of his taste and sensibility, was a man of humane studies and humane feelings, describes the refined and elegant manner in which the operation is performed, by way of mitigating the indignation which such a usage ought to excite. He assures us that the stamp is not a branding iron, but a silver instrument; and that it is heated not in the fire, but over the flame of spirits of wine.

Sir Thomas More.—Excellent planter! worthy to have been flogged at a gilt whipping-post with a scourge of gold thread! The practice of marking slaves had fallen into disuse; probably it was only used at first with captives, or with those who were newly-purchased from a distant country, never with those born upon the soil. And there was no means of raising a hue and cry after a runaway slave so effectually as is done by your colonial gazettes, the only productions of the British colonial press.

Montesinos.—Include, I pray you, in the former part of your censure the journals of the United States, the land of democracy and equal rights.

Sir Thomas More.—How much more honourable was the tendency of our laws, and of national feeling in those days, which you perhaps as well as your trans-Atlantic brethren have been accustomed to think barbarous, when compared with this your own age of reason and liberality! The master who killed his slave was as liable to punishment as if he had killed a freeman. Instead of impeding enfranchisement, the laws, as well as the public feeling, encouraged it. If a villein who had fled from his lord remained a year and a day unclaimed upon the King's demesne lands, or in any privileged town, he became free. All doubtful cases were decided in favorem libertatis. Even the established maxim in law, partus sequitur ventrem, was set aside in favour of liberty; the child of a neif was free if the father were a freeman, or if it were illegitimate, in which case it was settled that the free condition of the father should always be presumed.

Montesinos.—Such a principle must surely have tended to increase the illegitimate population.

Sir Thomas More.—That inference is drawn from the morals of your own age, and the pernicious effect of your poor laws as they are now thoroughly understood and deliberately acted upon by a race who are thinking always of their imaginary rights, and never of their duties. You forget the efficacy of ecclesiastical discipline; and that the old Church was more vigilant, and therefore more efficient than that which rose upon its ruins. And you suppose that personal liberty was more valued by persons in a state of servitude than was actually the case. For if in earlier ages emancipation was an act of piety and benevolence, afterwards, when the great crisis of society came on, it proceeded more frequently from avarice than from any worthier motive; and the slave who was set free sometimes found himself much in the situation of a household dog that is turned into the streets.

Montesinos.—Are you alluding to the progress of inclosures, which from the accession of the Tudors to the age of the Stuarts were complained of as the great and crying evil of the times?

Sir Thomas More.—That process originated as soon as rents began to be of more importance than personal services, and money more convenient to the landlords than payments in kind.

Montesinos.—And this I suppose began to be the case under Edward III. The splendour of his court, and the foreign wars in which he was engaged, must have made money more necessary to the knights and nobles than it had ever been before, except during the Crusades.

Sir Thomas More.—The wars of York and Lancaster retarded the process; but immediately after the termination of that fierce struggle it was accelerated by the rapid growth of commerce, and by the great influx of wealth from the new found world. Under a settled and strong and vigilant government men became of less value as vassals and retainers, because the boldest barons no longer dared contemplate the possibility of trying their strength against the crown, or attempting to disturb the succession. Four-legged animals therefore were wanted for slaughter more than two-legged ones; and moreover, sheep could be shorn, whereas the art of fleecing the tenantry was in its infancy, and could not always be practised with the same certain success. A trading spirit thus gradually superseded the rude but kindlier principle of the feudal system: profit and loss became the rule of conduct; in came calculation, and out went feeling.

Montesinos.—I remember your description (for indeed who can forget it?) how sheep, more destructive than the Dragon of Wantley in those days, began to devour men and fields and houses. The same process is at this day going on in the Highlands, though under different circumstances; some which palliate the evil, and some which aggravate the injustice.

Sir Thomas More.—The real nature of the evil was misunderstood by my contemporaries, and for some generations afterward. A decrease of population was the effect complained of, whereas the greater grievance was that a different and worse population was produced.

Montesinos.—I comprehend you. The same effect followed which has been caused in these days by the extinction of small farms.

Sir Thomas More.—The same in kind, but greater in degree; or at least if not greater, or so general in extent, it was more directly felt. When that ruinous fashion prevailed in your age there were many resources for the class of people who were thus thrown out of their natural and proper place in the social system. Your fleets and armies at that time required as many hands as could be supplied; and women and children were consumed with proportionate rapidity by your manufactures.

Moreover, there was the wholesome drain of emigration open

"Facta est immensi copia mundi."

But under the Tudors there existed no such means for disposing of the ejected population, and except the few who could obtain places as domestic servants, or employment as labourers and handicraftsmen (classes, it must be remembered, for all which the employ was diminished by the very ejectment in question), they who were turned adrift soon found themselves houseless and hopeless, and were reduced to prey upon that society which had so unwisely as well as inhumanly discarded them.

Montesinos.—Thus it is that men collectively as well as individually create for themselves so large a part of the evils they endure.

Sir Thomas More.—Enforce upon your contemporaries that truth which is as important in politics as in ethics, and you will not have lived in vain! Scatter that seed upon the waters, and doubt not of the harvest! Vindicate always the system of nature, in other and sounder words, the ways of God, while you point out with all faithfulness

"what ills
Remediable and yet unremedied
Afflict man's wretched race,"

and the approbation of your own heart will be sufficient reward on earth.

Montesinos.—The will has not been wanting.

Sir Thomas More.—There are cases in which the will carries with it the power; and this is of them. No man was ever yet deeply convinced of any momentous truth without feeling in himself the power as well as the desire of communicating it.

Montesinos.—True, Sir Thomas; but the perilous abuse of that feeling by enthusiasts and fanatics leads to an error in the opposite extreme.

We sacrifice too much to prudence; and, in fear of incurring the danger or the reproach of enthusiasm, too often we stifle the holiest impulses of the understanding and the heart.

"Our doubts are traitors,
And make us lose the good we oft might win,
By fearing to attempt."

- But I pray you, resume your discourse. The monasteries were probably the chief palliatives of this great evil while they existed.

Sir Thomas More.—Their power of palliating it was not great, for the expenditure of those establishments kept a just pace with their revenues. They accumulated no treasures, and never were any incomes more beneficially employed. The great abbeys vied with each other in architectural magnificence, in this more especially, but likewise in every branch of liberal expenditure, giving employment to great numbers, which was better than giving unearned food. They provided, as it became them, for the old and helpless also. That they prevented the necessity of raising rates for the poor by the copious alms which they distributed, and by indiscriminately feeding the indigent, has been inferred, because those rates became necessary immediately after the suppression of the religious houses. But this is one of those hasty inferences which have no other foundation than a mere coincidence of time in the supposed cause and effect.

Montesinos.—For which you have furnished a proverbial illustration in your excellent story of Tenterden Steeple and Goodwin Sands.

Sir Thomas More.—That illustration would have been buried in the dust if it had not been repeated by Hugh Latimer at St. Paul's Cross. It was the only thing in my writings by which he profited. If he had learnt more from them he might have died in his bed, with less satisfaction to himself and less honour from posterity. We went different ways, but we came to the same end, and met where we had little expectation of meeting. I must do him the justice to say that when he forwarded the work of destruction it was with the hope and intention of employing the materials in a better edifice; and that no man opposed the sacrilegious temper of the age more bravely. The monasteries, in the dissolution of which he rejoiced as much as he regretted the infamous disposal of their spoils, delayed the growth of pauperism, by the corrodies with which they were charged; the effect of these reservations on the part of the founders and benefactors being, that a comfortable and respectable support was provided for those who grew old in the service of their respective families; and there existed no great family, and perhaps no wealthy one, which had not entitled itself thus to dispose of some of its aged dependants. And the extent of the depopulating system was limited while those houses endured: because though some of the great abbots were not less rapacious than the lay lords, and more criminal, the heads in general could not be led, like the nobles, into a prodigal expenditure, the burthen of which fell always upon the tenants; and rents in kind were to them more convenient than in money, their whole economy being founded upon that system, and adapted to it.

Montesinos.—Both facts and arguments were indeed strongly on your side when you wrote against the supplication of beggars; but the form in which you embodied them gave the adversary an advantage, for it was connected with one of the greatest abuses and absurdities of the Romish Church.

Sir Thomas More.—Montesinos, I allow you to call it an abuse; but if you think any of the abuses of that church were in their origin so unreasonable as to deserve the appellation of absurdities, you must have studied its history with less consideration and a less equitable spirit than I have given you credit for. Both Master Fish and I had each our prejudices and errors. We were both sincere; Master Fish would undoubtedly have gone to the stake in defence of his opinions as cheerfully as I laid down my neck upon the block; like his namesake in the tale which you have quoted, he too when in Nix's frying-pan would have said he was in his duty, and content. But withal he cannot be called an honest man, unless in that sort of liberal signification by which, in these days, good words are so detorted from their original and genuine meaning as to express precisely the reverse of what was formerly intended by them. More gross exaggerations and more rascally mis-statements could hardly be made by one of your own thorough-paced revolutionists than those upon which the whole argument of his supplication is built.

Montesinos.—If he had fallen into your hands you would have made a stock-fish of him.

Sir Thomas More.—Perhaps so. I had not then I learnt that laying men by the heels is not the best way of curing them of an error in the head. But the

King protected him. Henry had too much sagacity not to perceive the consequences which such a book was likely to produce, and he said, after perusing it, "If a man should pull down an old stone wall, and begin at the bottom, the upper part thereof might chance to fall upon his head." But he saw also that it tended to serve his immediate purpose.

Montesinos.—I marvel that good old John Fox, upright, downright man as he was, should have inserted in his "Acts and Monuments" a libel like this, which contains no arguments except such as were adapted to ignorance, cupidity, and malice.

Sir Thomas More.—Old John Fox ought to have known that, however advantageous the dissolution of the monastic houses might be to the views of the Reformers, it was every way injurious to the labouring classes. As far as they were concerned, the transfer of property was always to worse hands. The tenantry were deprived of their best landlords, artificers of their best employers, the poor and miserable of their best and surest friends. There would have been no insurrections in behalf of the old religion if the zeal of the peasantry had not been inflamed by a sore feeling of the injury which they suffered in the change. A great increase of the vagabond population was the direct and immediate consequence. They who were ejected from their tenements or deprived of their accustomed employment were turned loose upon society; and the greater number, of course and of necessity, ran wild.

Montesinos.—Wild, indeed! The old chroniclers give a dreadful picture of their numbers and of their wickedness, which called forth and deserved the utmost severity of the law. They lived like savages in the woods and wastes, committing the most atrocious actions, stealing children, and burning, breaking, or otherwise disfiguring their limbs for the purpose of exciting compassion, and obtaining alms by this most flagitious of all imaginable crimes. Surely we have nothing so bad as this.

Sir Thomas More.—The crime of stealing children for such purposes is rendered exceedingly difficult by the ease and rapidity with which a hue and cry can now be raised throughout the land, and the eagerness and detestation with which the criminal would be pursued; still, however, it is sometimes practised. In other respects the professional beggars of the nineteenth century are not a whit better than their predecessors of the sixteenth; and your gipsies and travelling potters, who, gipsy-like, pitch their tents upon the common, or by the wayside, retain with as much fidelity the manners and morals of the old vagabonds as they do the cant, or pedlar's French, which this class of people are said to have invented in the age whereof we are now speaking.

Montesinos.—But the number of our vagabonds has greatly diminished. In your Henry's reign it is affirmed that no fewer than 72,000 criminals were hanged; you have yourself described them as strung up by scores upon a gibbet all over the country. Even in the golden days of good Queen Bess the executions were from three to four hundred annually. A large allowance must be made for the increased humanity of the nation, and the humaner temper with which the laws are administered: but the new crimes which increased wealth and a system of credit on one hand, and increased ingenuity, and new means of mischief on the part of the depredators have produced, must also be taken into the account. And the result will show a diminution in the number of those who prey upon society either by open war or secret wiles.

Sir Thomas More.—Add your paupers to the list, and you will then have added to it not less than an eighth of your whole population. But looking at the depredators alone, perhaps it will be found that the evil is at this time more widely extended, more intimately connected with the constitution of society, like a chronic and organic disease, and therefore more difficult of cure. Like other vermin they are numerous in proportion as they find shelter; and for this species of noxious beast large towns and manufacturing districts afford better cover than the forest or the waste. The fault lies in your institutions, which in the time of the Saxons were better adapted to maintain security and order than they are now. No man in those days could prey upon society unless he were at war with it as an outlaw, a proclaimed and open enemy. Rude as the laws were, the purposes of law had not then been perverted: it had not been made a craft; it served to deter men from committing crimes, or to punish them for the commission; never to shield notorious, acknowledged, impudent guilt from condign punishment. And in the fabric of society, imperfect as it was, the outline and rudiments of what it ought to be were distinctly marked in some main parts, where they are now well-nigh utterly effaced. Every person had his place. There was a system of superintendence everywhere, civil as well as religious. They who were born in villenage were born to an inheritance of labour, but not of inevitable depravity and wretchedness. If one class were regarded in some respects as cattle they were at least taken care of; they were trained, fed, sheltered and protected; and there was an eye upon them when they strayed. None were wild, unless they ran wild wilfully, and in defiance of control. None were beneath the notice of the priest, nor placed out of the possible reach of his instruction and his care. But how large a part of your population are like the dogs at Lisbon and Constantinople, unowned, unbroken to any useful purpose, subsisting by chance or by prey, living in filth, mischief, and wretchedness, a nuisance to the community while they live, and dying miserably at last! This evil had its beginning in my days; it is now approaching fast to its consummation.

COLLOQUY V

DECAY OF THE FEUDAL SYSTEM
EDWARD VI.—ALFRED

I had retired to my library as usual after dinner, and while I was wishing for the appearance of my ghostly visitor he became visible. "Behold me to your wish!" said he. "Thank you," I replied, "for those precious words."

Sir Thomas More.—Wherefore precious?

Montesinos.—Because they show that spirits who are in bliss perceive our thoughts;—that that communion with the departed for which the heart yearns in its moods of intensest feeling is in reality attained when it is desired.

Sir Thomas More.—You deduce a large inference from scanty premises. As if it were not easy to know without any super-human intuition that you would wish for the arrival of one whose company you like, at a time when you were expecting it.

Montesinos.—And is this all?

Sir Thomas More.—All that the words necessarily imply. For the rest, crede quod habeas et habes, according to the scurvy tale which makes my friend Erasmus a horse-stealer, and fathers Latin rhymes upon him. But let us take up the thread of our discourse, or, as we used to say in old times, "begin it again and mend it, for it is neither mass nor matins."

Montesinos.—You were saying that the evil of a vagrant and brutalised population began in your days, and is approaching to its consummation at this time.

Sir Thomas More.—The decay of the feudal system produced it. When armies were no longer raised upon that system soldiers were disbanded at the end of a war, as they are now: that is to say, they were turned adrift to fare as they could—to work if they could find employment; otherwise to beg, starve, live upon the alms of their neighbours, or prey upon a wider community in a manner more congenial to the habits and temper of their old vocation. In consequence of the gains which were to be obtained by inclosures and sheep-farming, families were unhoused and driven loose upon the country. These persons, and they who were emancipated from villenage, or who had in a more summary manner emancipated themselves, multiplied in poverty and wretchedness. Lastly, owing to the fashion for large households of retainers, great numbers of men were trained up in an idle and dissolute way of life, liable at any time to be cast off when age or accident invalided them, or when the master of the family died; and then if not ashamed to beg, too lewd to work, and ready for any kind of mischief. Owing to these co-operating causes, a huge population of outcasts was produced, numerous enough seriously to infest society, yet not so large as to threaten its subversion.

Montesinos.—A derangement of the existing system produced them then; they are a constituent part of the system now. With you they were, as you have called them, outcasts: with us, to borrow an illustration from foreign institutions, they have become a caste. But during two centuries the evil appears to have decreased. Why was this?

Sir Thomas More.—Because it was perceived to be an evil, and could never at any time be mistaken for a healthful symptom. And because circumstances tended to suspend its progress. The habits of these unhappy persons being at first wholly predatory, the laws proclaimed a sort of crusade against them, and great and inhuman riddance was made by the executioner. Foreign service opened a drain in the succeeding reigns: many also were drawn off by the spirit of maritime adventure, preferring the high seas to the high way, as a safer course of plundering. Then came an age of civil war, with its large demand for human life. Meanwhile as the old arrangements of society crumbled and decayed new ones were formed. The ancient fabric was repaired in some parts and modernised in others. And from the time of the Restoration the people supposed their institutions to be stable because after long and violent convulsions they found themselves at rest, and the transition which was then going on was slow, silent, and unperceived. The process of converting slaves and villeins into servants and free peasantry had ended; that of raising a manufacturing populace and converting peasantry into poor was but begun; and it proceeded slowly for a full hundred years.

Montesinos.—Those hundred years were the happiest which England has ever known.

Sir Thomas More.—Perhaps so: [Greek text which cannot be reproduced]

Montesinos.—With the exception of the efforts which were made for restoring the exiled family of the Stuarts they were years of quiet uniform prosperity and advancement. The morals of the country recovered from the contagion which Charles II. imported from France, and for which Puritanism had prepared the people. Visitations of pestilence were suspended. Sectarians enjoyed full toleration, and were contented. The Church proved itself worthy of the victory which it had obtained. The Constitution, after one great but short struggle, was well balanced and defined; and if the progress of art, science, and literature was not brilliant, it was steady, and the way for a brighter career was prepared.

Sir Thomas More.—The way was prepared meantime for evil as well as for good. You were retrograde in sound policy, sound philosophy and sound learning. Our business at present is wholly with the first. Because your policy, defective as it was at the best, had been retrograde, discoveries in physics, and advances in mechanical science which would have produced nothing but good in Utopia, became as injurious to the weal of the nation as they were instrumental to its wealth. But such had your system imperceptibly become, and such were your statesmen, that the wealth of nations was considered as the sole measure of their prosperity.

Montesinos.—In feudal ages the object of those monarchs who had any determinate object in view was either to extend their dominions by conquest from their neighbours, or to increase their authority at home by breaking the power of a turbulent nobility. In commercial ages the great and sole object of government, when not engaged in war, was to augment its revenues, for the purpose of supporting the charges which former wars had induced, or which the apprehension of fresh ones rendered necessary. And thus it has been, that of the two main ends of government, which are the security of the subjects and the improvement of the nation, the latter has never been seriously attempted, scarcely indeed taken into consideration; and the former imperfectly attained.

Sir Thomas More.—Fail not, however, I entreat you, to bear in mind that this has not been the fault of your rulers at any time. It has been their misfortune—an original sin in the constitution of the society wherein they were born. Circumstances which they did not make and could not control have impelled them onward in ways which neither for themselves nor the nation were ways of pleasantness and peace.

Montesinos.—There is one beautiful exception—Edward VI.

"That blessed Prince whose saintly name might move The understanding heart to tears of reverent love."

He would have struck into the right course.

Sir Thomas More.—You have a Catholic feeling concerning saints, Montesinos, though you look for them in the Protestant calendar. Edward deserves to be remembered with that feeling. But had his life been prolonged to the full age of man it would not have been in his power to remedy the evil which had been done in his father's reign and during his own minority. To have effected that would have required a strength and obduracy of character incompatible with his meek and innocent nature. In intellect and attainments he kept pace with his age, a more stirring and intellectual one than any which had gone before it: but in the wisdom of the heart he was far beyond that age, or indeed any that has succeeded it. It cannot be said of him as of Henry of Windsor, that he was fitter for a cloister than a throne, but he was fitter for a heavenly crown than a terrestrial one. This country was not worthy of him!— scarcely this earth!

Montesinos.—There is a homely verse common in village churchyards, the truth of which has been felt by many a heart, as some consolation in its keenest afflictions:-

"God calls them first whom He loves best."

But surely no prince ever more sedulously employed himself to learn his office. His views in some respects were not in accord with the more enlarged principles of trade, which experience has taught us. But on the other hand he judged rightly what "the medicines were by which the sores of the commonwealth might be healed." His prescriptions are as applicable now as they were then, and in most points as needful: they were "good education, good example, good laws, and the just execution of those laws: punishing the vagabond and idle, encouraging the good, ordering well the customers, and engendering friendship in all parts of the commonwealth." In these, and more especially in the first of these, he hoped and purposed to have "shown his device." But it was not permitted. Nevertheless, he has his reward. It has been more wittily than charitably said that Hell is paved with good intentions: they have their place in Heaven also. Evil thoughts and desires are justly accounted to us for sin; assuredly therefore the sincere goodwill will be accounted for the deed, when means and opportunity have been wanting to bring it to effect. There are feelings and purposes as well as "thoughts,

> - whose very sweetness yieldeth proof
> That they were born for immortality."

Sir Thomas More.—Those great legislative measures whereby the character of a nation is changed and stamped are more practicable in a barbarous age than in one so far advanced as that of the Tudors; under a despotic government, than under a free one; and among an ignorant, rather than inquiring people. Obedience is then either yielded to a power which is too strong to be resisted, or willingly given to the acknowledged superiority of some commanding mind, carrying with it, as in such ages it does, an appearance of divinity. Our incomparable Alfred was a prince in many respects favourably circumstanced for accomplishing a great work like this, if his victory over the Danes had been so complete as to have secured the country against any further evils from that tremendous enemy. And had England remained free from the scourge of their invasion under his successors, it is more than likely that his institutions would at this day have been the groundwork of your polity.

Montesinos.—If you allude to that part of the Saxon law which required that all the people should be placed under borh, I must observe that even those writers who regard the name of Alfred with the greatest reverence always condemn this part of his system of government.

Sir Thomas More.—It is a question of degree. The just medium between too much superintendence and too little: the mystery whereby the free will of the subject is preserved, while it is directed by the fore purpose of the State (which is the secret of true polity), is yet to be found out. But this is certain, that whatever be the origin of government, its duties are patriarchal, that is to say, parental: superintendence is one of those duties, and is capable of being exercised to any extent by delegation and sub-delegation.

Montesinos.—The Madras system, my excellent friend Dr. Bell would exclaim if he were here. That which, as he says, gives in a school to the master, the hundred eyes of Argus, and the hundred hands of Briareus, might in a state give omnipresence to law, and omnipotence to order. This is indeed the fair ideal of a commonwealth.

Sir Thomas More.—And it was this at which Alfred aimed. His means were violent, because the age was barbarous. Experience would have shown wherein they required amendment, and as manners improved the laws would have been softened with them. But they disappeared altogether during the years of internal warfare and turbulence which ensued. The feudal order which was established with the Norman conquest, or at least methodised after it, was in this part of its scheme less complete: still it had the same bearing. When that also went to decay, municipal police did not supply its place. Church discipline then fell into disuse; clerical influence was lost; and the consequence now is, that in a country where one part of the community enjoys the highest advantages of civilisation with which any people upon this globe have ever in any age been favoured, there is among the lower classes a mass of ignorance, vice, and wretchedness, which no generous heart can contemplate without grief, and which, when the other signs of the times are considered, may reasonably excite alarm for the fabric of society that rests upon such a base. It resembles the tower in your own vision, its beautiful summit elevated above all other buildings, the foundations placed upon the sand, and mouldering.

Montesinos.

"Rising so high, and built so insecure,
Ill may such perishable work endure!"

You will not, I hope, come to that conclusion! You will not, I hope, say with the evil prophet -

"The fabric of her power is undermined;
The Earthquake underneath it will have way,
And all that glorious structure, as the wind
Scatters a summer cloud, be swept away!"

Sir Thomas More.—Look at the populace of London, and ask yourself what security there is that the same blind fury which broke out in your childhood against the Roman Catholics may not be excited against the government, in one of those opportunities which accident is perpetually offering to the desperate villains whom your laws serve rather to protect than to punish!

Montesinos.—It is an observation of Mercier's, that despotism loves large cities. The remark was made with reference to Paris only a little while before the French Revolution! But even if he had looked no farther than the history of his own country and of that very metropolis, he might have found sufficient proof that insubordination and anarchy like them quite as well.

Sir Thomas More.—London is the heart of your commercial system, but it is also the hot-bed of corruption. It is at once the centre of wealth and the sink of misery; the seat of intellect and empire: and yet a wilderness wherein they, who live like wild beasts upon their fellow-creatures, find prey and cover. Other wild beasts have long since been extirpated: even in the wilds of Scotland, and of barbarous, or worse than barbarous Ireland, the wolf is no longer to be found; a degree of civilisation this to which no other country has attained. Man, and man alone, is permitted to run wild. You plough your fields and harrow them; you have your scarifiers to make the ground clean; and if after all this weeds should spring up, the careful cultivator roots them out by hand. But ignorance and misery and vice are allowed to grow, and blossom, and seed, not on the waste alone, but in the very garden and pleasure-ground of society and civilisation. Old Thomas Tusser's coarse remedy is the only one which legislators have yet thought of applying.

Montesinos.—What remedy is that?

Sir Thomas More.—'Twas the husbandman's practice in his days and mine:

"Where plots full of nettles annoyeth the eye,
Sow hempseed among them, and nettles will die."

Montesinos.—The use of hemp indeed has not been spared. But with so little avail has it been used, or rather to such ill effect, that every public execution, instead of deterring villains from guilt, serves only to afford them opportunity for it. Perhaps the very risk of the gallows operates upon many a man among the inducements to commit the crime whereto he is tempted; for with your true gamester the excitement seems to be in proportion to the value of the stake. Yet I hold as little with the humanity-mongers, who deny the necessity and lawfulness of inflicting capital punishment in any case, as with the shallow moralists, who exclaim against vindictive justice, when punishment would cease to be just, if it were not vindictive.

Sir Thomas More.—And yet the inefficacious punishment of guilt is less to be deplored and less to be condemned than the total omission of all means for preventing it. Many thousands in your metropolis rise every morning without knowing how they are to subsist during the day, or many of them where they are to lay their heads at night. All men, even the vicious themselves, know that wickedness leads to misery; but many, even among the good and the wise, have yet to learn that misery is almost as often the cause of wickedness.

Montesinos.—There are many who know this, but believe that it is not in the power of human institutions to prevent this misery. They see the effect, but regard the causes as inseparable from the condition of human nature.

Sir Thomas More.—As surely as God is good, so surely there is no such thing as necessary evil. For by the religious mind sickness and pain and death are not to be accounted evils. Moral evils are of your own making, and undoubtedly the greater part of them may be prevented; though it is only in Paraguay (the most imperfect of Utopias) that any attempt at prevention has been carried into effect. Deformities of mind, as of body, will sometimes occur. Some voluntary castaways there will always be, whom no fostering kindness and no parental care can preserve from self-destruction; but if any are lost for want of care and culture, there is a sin of omission in the society to which they belong.

Montesinos.—The practicability of forming such a system of prevention may easily be allowed, where, as in Paraguay, institutions are fore-planned, and not, as everywhere in Europe, the slow and varying growth of circumstances. But to introduce it into an old society, hic labor, hoc opus est! The Augean stable might have been kept clean by ordinary labour, if from the first the filth had been removed every day; when it had accumulated for years, it became a task for Hercules to cleanse it. Alas, the age of heroes and demigods is over!

Sir Thomas More.—There lies your error! As no general will ever defeat an enemy whom he believes to be invincible, so no difficulty can be overcome by those who fancy themselves unable to overcome it. Statesmen in this point are, like physicians, afraid, lest their own reputation should suffer, to try new remedies in cases where the old routine of practice is known and proved to be ineffectual. Ask yourself whether the wretched creatures of whom we are discoursing are not abandoned to their fate without the highest attempt to rescue them from it? The utmost which your laws profess is, that under their administration no human being shall perish for want: this is all! To effect this you draw from the wealthy, the industrious, and the frugal, a revenue exceeding tenfold the whole expenses of government under Charles I., and yet even with this enormous expenditure upon the poor it is not effected. I say nothing of those who perish for want of sufficient food and necessary comforts, the victims of slow suffering and obscure disease; nor of those who, having crept to some brick-kiln at night, in hope of preserving life by its warmth, are found there dead in the morning. Not a winter passes in which some poor wretch does not actually die of cold and hunger in the streets of London! With all your public and private eleemosynary establishments, with your eight million of poor-rates, with your numerous benevolent associations, and with a spirit of charity in individuals which keeps pace with the wealth of the richest nation in the world, these things happen, to the disgrace of the age and country, and to the opprobrium of humanity, for want of police and order! You are silent!

Montesinos.—Some shocking examples occurred to me. The one of a poor Savoyard boy with his monkey starved to death in St. James's Park. The other, which is, if that be possible, a still more disgraceful case, is recorded incidentally in Rees's Cyclopaedia under the word "monster." It is only in a huge overgrown city that such cases could possibly occur.

Sir Thomas More.—The extent of a metropolis ought to produce no such consequences. Whatever be the size of a bee-hive or an ant- hill, the same perfect order is observed in it.

Montesinos.—That is because bees and ants act under the guidance of unerring instinct.

Sir Thomas More.—As if instinct were a superior faculty to reason! But the statesman, as well as the sluggard, may be told to "go to the ant and the bee, consider their ways and be wise!" It is for reason to observe and profit by the examples which instinct affords it.

Montesinos.—A country modelled upon Apiarian laws would be a strange Utopia! the bowstring would be used there as unmercifully as it is in the seraglio, to say nothing of the summary mode of bringing down the population to the means of subsistence. But this is straying from the subject. The consequences of defective order are indeed frightful, whether we regard the physical or the moral evils which are produced

Sir Thomas More.—And not less frightful when the political evils are contemplated. To the dangers of an oppressive and iniquitous order, such, for example, as exists where negro slavery is established, you are fully awake in England; but to those of defective order among yourselves, though they are precisely of the same nature, you are blind. And yet you have spirits among you who are labouring day and night to stir up a bellum servile, an insurrection like that of Wat Tyler, of the Jacquerie, and of the peasants in Germany. There is no provocation for this, as there was in all those dreadful convulsions of society: but there are misery and ignorance and desperate wickedness to work upon, which the want of order has produced. Think for a moment what London, nay, what the whole kingdom would be, were your Catilines to succeed in exciting as general an insurrection as that which was raised by one madman in your own childhood! Imagine the infatuated and infuriated wretches, whom not

Spitalfields, St. Giles's, and Pimlico alone, but all the lanes and alleys and cellars of the metropolis would pour out—a frightful population, whose multitudes, when gathered together, might almost exceed belief! The streets of London would appear to teem with them, like the land of Egypt with its plague of frogs: and the lava floods from a volcano would be less destructive than the hordes whom your great cities and manufacturing districts would vomit forth!

Montesinos.—Such an insane rebellion would speedily be crushed.

Sir Thomas More.—Perhaps so. But three days were enough for the Fire of London. And be assured this would not pass away without leaving in your records a memorial as durable and more dreadful.

Montesinos.—Is such an event to be apprehended?

Sir Thomas More.—Its possibility at least ought always to be borne in mind. The French Revolution appeared much less possible when the Assembly of Notables was convoked; and the people of France were much less prepared for the career of horrors into which they were presently hurried.

COLLOQUY VI

THE LIBRARY

I was in my library, making room upon the shelves for some books which had just arrived from New England, removing to a less conspicuous station others which were of less value and in worse dress, when Sir Thomas entered. You are employed, said he, to your heart's content. Why, Montesinos, with these books, and the delight you take in their constant society, what have you to covet or desire?

Montesinos.—Nothing, except more books.

Sir Thomas More. -

"Crescit, indulgens sibi, dirus hydrops."

Montesinos.—Nay, nay, my ghostly monitor, this at least is no diseased desire. If I covet more, it is for the want I feel and the use which I should make of them. "Libraries," says my good old friend George Dyer, a man as learned as he is benevolent, "libraries are the wardrobes of literature, whence men, properly informed, might bring forth something for ornament, much for curiosity, and more for use." These books of mine, as you well know, are not drawn up here for display, however much the pride of the eye may be gratified in beholding them, they are on actual service. Whenever they may be dispersed, there is not one among them that will ever be more comfortably lodged, or more highly prized by its possessor; and generations may pass away before some of them will again find a reader. It is well that we do not moralise too much upon such subjects.

"For foresight is a melancholy gift,
Which bares the bald, and speeds the all-too-swift."

H. T.

But the dispersion of a library, whether in retrospect or in anticipation, is always to me a melancholy thing.

Sir Thomas More.—How many such dispersions must have taken place to have made it possible that these books should thus be brought together here among the Cumberland mountains.

Montesinos.—Many, indeed; and in many instances most disastrous ones. Not a few of these volumes have been cast up from the wreck of the family or convent libraries during the late Revolution. Yonder "Acta Sanctorum" belonged to the Capuchins, at Ghent. This book of St. Bridget's Revelations, in which not only all the initial letters are illuminated, but every capital throughout the volume was coloured, came from the Carmelite Nunnery at Bruges. That copy of Alain Chartier, from the Jesuits' College at Louvain; that Imago Primi Saeculi Societatis, from their college at Ruremond. Here are books from Colbert's library, here others from the Lamoignon one. And here are two volumes of a work, not more rare than valuable for its contents, divorced, unhappily, and it is to be feared for ever, from the one which should stand between them; they were printed in a convent at Manila, and brought from thence when that city was taken by Sir William Draper; they have given me, perhaps, as many pleasurable hours (passed in acquiring information which I could not otherwise have obtained), as Sir William spent years of anxiety and vexation in vainly soliciting the reward of his conquest.

About a score of the more out-of-the-way works in my possession belonged to some unknown person, who seems carefully to have gleaned the bookstalls a little before and after the year 1790. He marked them with certain ciphers, always at the end of the volume. They are in various languages, and I never found his mark in any book that was not worth buying, or that I should not have bought without that indication to induce me. All were in ragged condition, and having been dispersed, upon the owner's death probably, as of no value, to the stalls they had returned; and there I found this portion of them just before my old haunts as a book-hunter in the metropolis were disforested, to make room for the improvements between Westminster and Oxford Road. I have endeavoured without success to discover the name of their former possessor. He must have been a remarkable man, and the whole of his collection, judging of it by that part which has come into my hands, must have been singularly curious. A book is the more valuable to me when I know to whom it has belonged, and through what "scenes and changes" it has passed.

Sir Thomas More.—You would have its history recorded in the fly- leaf as carefully as the pedigree of a racehorse is preserved.

Montesinos.—I confess that I have much of that feeling in which the superstition concerning relics has originated, and I am sorry when I see the name of a former owner obliterated in a book, or the plate of his arms defaced. Poor memorials though they be, yet they are something saved for a while from oblivion, and I should be almost as unwilling to destroy them as to efface the Hic jacet of a tombstone. There may be sometimes a pleasure in recognising them, sometimes a salutary sadness.

Yonder Chronicle of King D. Manoel, by Damiam de Goes, and yonder "General History of Spain," by Esteban de Garibay, are signed by their respective authors. The minds of these laborious and useful scholars are in their works, but you are brought into a more personal relation with them when you see the page upon which you know that their eyes have rested, and the very characters which their hands have traced. This copy of Casaubon's Epistles was sent to me from Florence by Walter Landor. He had perused it carefully, and to that perusal we are indebted for one of the most pleasing of his Conversations; these letters had carried him in spirit to the age of their writer, and shown James I. to him in the light wherein James was regarded by contemporary scholars, and under the impression thus produced Landor has written of him in his happiest mood, calmly, philosophically, feelingly, and with no more of favourable leaning than justice will always manifest when justice is in good humour and in charity with all men. The book came from the palace library at Milan, how or when abstracted I know not, but this beautiful dialogue would never have been written had it remained there in its place upon the shelf, for the worms to finish the work which they had begun. Isaac Casaubon must be in your society, Sir

Thomas, for where Erasmus is you will be, and there also Casaubon will have his place among the wise and the good. Tell him, I pray you, that due honour has in these days been rendered to his name by one who as a scholar is qualified to appreciate his merits, and whose writings will be more durable than monuments of brass or marble.

Sir Thomas More.—Is there no message to him from Walter Landor's friend?

Montesinos.—Say to him, since you encourage me to such boldness, that his letters could scarcely have been perused with deeper interest by the persons to whom they were addressed than they have been by one, at the foot of Skiddaw, who is never more contentedly employed than when learning from the living minds of other ages, one who would gladly have this expression of respect and gratitude conveyed to him, and who trusts that when his course is finished here he shall see him face to face.

Here is a book with which Lauderdale amused himself, when Cromwell kept him prisoner in Windsor Castle. He has recorded his state of mind during that imprisonment by inscribing in it, with his name, and the dates of time and place, the Latin word Durate, and the Greek [Greek text which cannot be reproduced]. Here is a memorial of a different kind inscribed in this "Rule of Penance of St. Francis, as it in ordered for religious women." "I beseech my deare mother humbly to accept of this exposition of our holy rule, the better to conceive what your poor child ought to be, who daly beges your blessing. Constantia Francisco." And here in the Apophthegmata, collected by Conrad Lycosthenes, and published after drastic expurgation by the Jesuits as a commonplace book, some Portuguese has entered a hearty vow that he would never part with the book, nor lend it to any one. Very different was the disposition of my poor old Lisbon acquaintance, the Abbe, who, after the old humaner form, wrote in all his books (and he had a rare collection) Ex libris Francisci Garnier, et amicorum.

Sir Thomas More.—How peaceably they stand together—Papists and Protestants side by side.

Montesinos.—Their very dust reposes not more quietly in the cemetery. Ancient and modern, Jew and Gentile, Mahommedan and Crusader, French and English, Spaniards and Portuguese, Dutch and Brazilians, fighting their own battles, silently now, upon the same shelf: Fernam Lopez and Pedro de Ayala; John de Laet and Barlaeus, with the historians of Joam Fernandes Vieira; Foxe's Martyrs and the Three Conversions of Father Parsons; Cranmer and Stephen Gardiner; Dominican and Franciscan; Jesuit and Philosophe (equally misnamed); Churchmen and Sectarians; Round-heads and Cavaliers

> "Here are God's conduits, grave divines; and here
> Is Nature's secretary, the philosopher:
> And wily statesmen, which teach how to tie
> The sinews of a city's mystic body;
> Here gathering chroniclers; and by them stand
> Giddy fantastic poets of each land."—DONNE.

Here I possess these gathered treasures of time, the harvest of so many generations, laid up in my garners: and when I go to the window there is the lake, and the circle of the mountains, and the illimitable sky.

Sir Thomas More.—"Felicemque voco pariter studiique locique!"

Montesinos.—"—meritoque probas artesque locumque."

The simile of the bees,

"Sic vos non vobis mellificatis apes,"

has often been applied to men who have made literature their profession; and they among them to whom worldly wealth and worldly honours are objects of ambition, may have reason enough to acknowledge its applicability. But it will bear a happier application and with equal fitness: for, for whom is the purest honey hoarded that the bees of this world elaborate, if it be not for the man of letters? The exploits of the kings and heroes of old, serve now to fill story-books for his amusement and instruction. It was to delight his leisure and call forth his admiration that Homer sung and Alexander conquered. It is to gratify his curiosity that adventurers have traversed deserts and savage countries, and navigators have explored the seas from pole to pole. The revolutions of the planet which he inhabits are but matters for his speculation; and the deluges and conflagrations which it has undergone, problems to exercise his philosophy, or fancy. He is the inheritor of whatever has been discovered by persevering labour, or created by inventive genius. The wise of all ages have heaped up a treasure for him, which rust doth not corrupt, and which thieves cannot break through and steal. I must leave out the moth, for even in this climate care is required against its ravages.

Sir Thomas More.—Yet, Montesinos, how often does the worm-eaten volume outlast the reputation of the worm-eaten author!

Montesinos.—Of the living one also; for many there are of whom it may be said, in the words of Vida, that -

"—ipsi

Saepe suis superant monumentis; illaudatique

Extremum ante diem faetus flevere caducos,

Viventesque suae viderunt funera famae."

Some literary reputations die in the birth; a few are nibbled to death by critics, but they are weakly ones that perish thus, such only as must otherwise soon have come to a natural death. Somewhat more numerous are those which are overfed with praise, and die of the surfeit. Brisk reputations, indeed, are like bottled twopenny, or pop "they sparkle, are exhaled, and fly"—not to heaven, but to the Limbo. To live among books, is in this respect like living among the tombs; you have in them speaking remembrancers of mortality. "Behold this also is vanity!"

Sir Thomas More.—Has it proved to you "vexation of spirit" also?

Montesinos.—Oh, no! for never can any man's life have been passed more in accord with his own inclinations, nor more answerably to his own desires. Excepting that peace which, through God's infinite mercy, is derived from a higher source, it is to literature, humanly speaking, that I am beholden, not only for the means of subsistence, but for every blessing which I enjoy; health of mind and activity of mind, contentment, cheerfulness, continual employment, and therewith continual pleasure. Sua vissima vita indies, sentire se fieri meliorem; and this as Bacon has said, and Clarendon repeated, is the benefit that a studious man enjoys in retirement. To the studies which I have faithfully pursued I am indebted for friends with whom, hereafter, it will be deemed an honour to have lived in friendship; and as for the enemies which they have procured to me in sufficient numbers, happily I am not of the thin-skinned race: they might as well fire small-shot at a rhinoceros, as direct their attacks upon me. In omnibus requiem quaesivi, said Thomas a Kempis, sed non inveni nisi in angulis et libellis. I too have found repose where he did, in books and retirement, but it was there alone I sought it: to these my nature, under the direction of a merciful Providence, led me betimes, and the world can offer nothing which should tempt me from them.

Sir Thomas More.—If wisdom were to be found in the multitude of books, what a progress must this nation have made in it since my head was cut off! A man in my days might offer to dispute de omni scibile, and in accepting the challenge I, as a young man, was not guilty of any extraordinary presumption, for all which books could teach was, at that time, within the compass of a diligent and ardent student. Even then we had difficulties to contend with which were unknown to the ancients. The curse of Babel fell lightly upon them. The Greeks despised other nations too much to think of acquiring their languages for the love of knowledge, and the Romans contented themselves with learning only the Greek. But tongues which, in my lifetime, were hardly formed, have since been refined and cultivated, and are become fertile in authors; and others, the very names of which were then unknown in Europe, have been discovered and mastered by European scholars, and have been found rich in literature. The circle of knowledge has thus widened in every generation; and you cannot now touch the circumference of what might formerly have been clasped.

Montesinos.—We are fortunate, methinks, who live in an age when books are accessible and numerous, and yet not so multiplied, as to render a competent, not to say thorough, acquaintance with any one branch of literature, impossible. He has it yet in his power to know much, who can be contented to remain in ignorance of more, and to say with Scaliger, non sum ex illis gloriosulis qui nihil ignorant.

Sir Thomas More.—If one of the most learned men whom the world has ever seen felt it becoming in him to say this two centuries ago, how infinitely smaller in these days must the share of learning which the most indefatigable student can hope to attain, be in proportion to what he must wish to learn! The sciences are simplified as they are improved; old rubbish and demolished fabrics serve there to make a foundation for new scaffolding, and more enduring superstructures; and every discoverer in physics bequeaths to those who follow him greater advantages than he possessed at the commencement of his labours. The reverse of this is felt in all the higher branches of literature. You have to acquire what the learned of the last age acquired, and in addition to it, what they themselves have added to the stock of learning. Thus the task is greater in every succeeding generation, and in a very few more it must become manifestly impossible.

Montesinos. Pope Ganganelli is said to have expressed a whimsical opinion that all the books in the world might be reduced to six thousand volumes in folio—by epitomising, expurgating, and destroying whatever the chosen and plenipotential committee of literature should in their wisdom think proper to condemn. It is some consolation to know that no Pope, or Nero, or Bonaparte, however great their power, can ever think such a scheme sufficiently within the bounds of possibility for them to dream of attempting it; otherwise the will would not be wanting. The evil which you anticipate is already perceptible in its effects. Well would it be if men were as moderate in their desire of wealth, as those who enter the ranks of literature, and lay claim to distinction there, are in their desire of knowledge! A slender capital suffices to begin with, upon the strength of which they claim credit, and obtain it as readily as their fellow adventurers in trade. If they succeed in setting up a present reputation, their ambition extends no further. The very vanity which finds its present food produces in them a practical contempt for any fame beyond what they can live to enjoy; and this sense of its insignificance to themselves is what better minds hardly attain, even in their saddest wisdom, till this world darkens upon them, and they feel that they are on the confines of eternity. But every age has had its sciolists, and will continue to have them; and in every age literature has also had, and will continue to have its sincere and devoted followers, few in number, but enough to trim the everlasting lamp. It is when sciolists meddle with State affairs that they become the pests of a nation; and this evil, for the reason which you have assigned, is more likely to increase than to be diminished. In your days all extant history lay within compassable bounds: it is a fearful thing to consider now what length of time would be required to make studious man as conversant with the history of Europe since those days, as he ought to be, if he would be properly qualified for holding a place in the councils of a kingdom. Men who take the course of public life will not, nor can they be expected to, wait for this. Youth and ardour, and ambition and impatience, are here in accord with worldly prudence; if they would reach the goal for which they start, they must begin the career betimes; and such among them as may be conscious that their stock of knowledge is less than it ought to be for such a profession, would not hesitate on that account to take an active part in public affairs, because they have a more comfortable consciousness that they are quite as well informed as the contemporaries, with whom they shall have to act, or to contend. The quantulum at which Oxenstern admired would be a large allowance now. For any such person to suspect himself of deficiency would, in this age of pretension, be a hopeful symptom; but should he endeavour to supply it, he is like a mail-coach traveller, who is to be conveyed over macadamised roads at the rate of nine miles an hour, including stoppages, and must therefore take at his minuted meals whatever food is readiest. He must get information for immediate use, and with the smallest cost of time; and therefore it is sought in abstracts and epitomes, which afford meagre food to the intellect, though they take away the uneasy sense of inanition. Tout abrege sur un bon livre est un sot abrege, says Montaigne; and of all abridgments there are none by which a reader is liable, and so likely, to be deceived as by epitomised histories.

Sir Thomas More.—Call to mind, I pray you, my foliophagous friend, what was the extent of Michael Montaigne's library; and that if you had passed a winter in his chateau you must, with that appetite of yours, have but yourself upon short allowance there. Historical knowledge is not the first thing needful for a statesman, nor the second. And yet do not hastily conclude that I am about to disparage its importance. A sailor might as well put to sea without chart or compass as a minister venture to steer the ship of the State without it. For as "the strong and strange varieties" in human nature are repeated in every age, so "the thing which hath been, it is that which shall be. Is there anything whereof it may be said, See, this is new? it hath been already of old time which was before us."

Montesinos.—"For things forepast are precedents to us, Whereby we may things present now, discuss,"as the old poet said who brought together a tragical collection of precedents in the mirror of magistrates. This is what Lord Brooke calls

"the second light of government
Which stories yield, and no time can disseason:"
"the common standard of man's reason," he holds to be the first light which the founders of a new state, or the governors of an old one, ought to follow.

Sir Thomas More.—Rightly, for though the most sagacious author that ever deduced maxims of policy from the experience of former ages has said that the misgovernment of States, and the evils consequent thereon, have arisen more from the neglect of that experience—that is, from historical ignorance—than from any other cause, the sum and substance of historical knowledge for practical purposes consists in certain general principles; and he who understands those principles, and has a due sense of their importance, has always, in the darkest circumstances, a star in sight by which he may direct his course surely.

Montesinos.—The British ministers who began and conducted the first war against revolutionary France, were once reminded, in a memorable speech, that if they had known, or knowing had borne in mind, three maxims of Machiavelli, they would not have committed the errors which cost this country so dearly. They would not have relied upon bringing the war to a successful end by aid of a party among the French: they would not have confided in the reports of emigrants; and they would not have supposed that because the French finances were in confusion, France was therefore incapable of carrying on war with vigour and ability; men and not money being the sinews of war, as Machiavelli had taught, and the revolutionary rulers and Buonaparte after them had learnt. Each of these errors they committed, though all were marked upon the chart!

Sir Thomas More.—Such maxims are like beacons on a dangerous shore, not the less necessary, because the seaman may sometimes be deceived by false lights, and sometimes mistaken in his distances; but the possibility of being so misled will be borne in mind by the cautious. Machiavelli is always sagacious, but the tree of knowledge of which he had gathered grew not in Paradise; it had a bitter root, and the fruit savours thereof, even to deadliness. He believed men to be so malignant by nature that they always act malevolently from choice, and never well except by compulsion, a devilish doctrine, to be accounted for rather than excused by the circumstances of his age and country. For he lived in a land where intellect was highly cultivated, and morals thoroughly corrupted, the Papal Church having by its doctrines, its practices, and its example, made one part of the Italians heathenism and superstitious, the other impious, and both wicked.

The rule of policy as well as of private morals is to be found in the Gospel; and a religious sense of duty towards God and man is the first thing needful in a statesman: herein he has an unerring guide when knowledge fails him, and experience affords no light. This, with a clear head and a single heart, will carry him through all difficulties; and the just confidence which, having these, he will then have in himself, will obtain for him the confidence of the nation. In every nation, indeed, which is conscious of its strength, the minister who takes the highest tone will invariably be the most popular; let him uphold, even haughtily, the character of his country, and the heart and voice of the people will be with him. But haughtiness implies always something that is hollow: the tone of a wise minister will be firm but calm. He will neither truckle to his enemies in the vain hope of conciliating them by a specious candour, which they at the same time flatter and despise; nor will he stand aloof from his friends, lest he should be accused of regarding them with partiality; and thus while he secures the attachment of the one he will command the respect of the other. He will not, like the Lacedemonians, think any measures honourable which accord with his inclinations, and just if they promote his views; but in all cases he will do that which is lawful and right, holding this for a certain truth, that in politics the straight path is the sure one! Such a minister will hope for the best, and expect the best; by acting openly, steadily, and bravely, he will act always for the best: and so acting, be the issue what it may, he will never dishonour himself or his country, nor fall under the "sharp judgment" of which they that are in "high places" are in danger.

Montesinos.—I am pleased to hear you include hopefulness among the needful qualifications.

Sir Thomas More.—It was a Jewish maxim that the spirit of prophecy rests only upon eminent, happy, and cheerful men.

Montesinos.—A wise woman, by which I do not mean in vulgar parlance one who pretends to prophecy, has a maxim to the same effect: Toma este aviso, she says, guardate de aquel que no tiene esperanza de bien! take care of him who hath no hope of good!

Sir Thomas More.—"Of whole heart cometh hope," says old Piers Plowman. And these maxims are warranted by philosophy, divine and human; by human wisdom, because he who hopes little will attempt little—fear is "a betrayal of the succours which reason offereth," and in difficult times, pericula magna non nisi periculis depelli solent; by religion, because the ways of providence are not so changed under the dispensation of Grace from what they were under the old law but that he who means well, and acts well, and is not wanting to himself, may rightfully look for a blessing upon the course which he pursues. The upright individual may rest his heal in peace upon this hope; the upright minister who conducts the affairs of a nation may trust in it; for as national sins bring after them in sure consequence their merited punishment, so national virtue, which is national wisdom, obtains in like manner its temporal and visible reward.

Blessings and curses are before you, and which are to be your portion depends upon the direction of public opinion. The march of intellect is proceeding at quick time; and if its progress be not accompanied by a corresponding improvement in morals and religion, the faster it proceeds, with the more violence will you be hurried down the road to ruin.

One of the first effects of printing was to make proud men look upon learning as disgraced by being thus brought within reach of the common people. Till that time learning, such as it was, had been confined to courts and convents, the low birth of the clergy being overlooked because they were privileged by their order. But when laymen in humble life were enabled to procure books the pride of aristocracy took an absurd course, insomuch that at one time it was deemed derogatory for a nobleman if he could read or write. Even scholars themselves complained that the reputation of learning, and the respect due to it, and its rewards were lowered when it was thrown open to all men; and it was seriously proposed to prohibit the printing of any book that could be afforded for sale below the price of three soldi. This base and invidious feeling was perhaps never so directly avowed in other countries as in Italy, the land where literature was first restored; and yet in this more liberal island ignorance was for some generations considered to be a mark of distinction, by which a man of gentle birth chose, not unfrequently, to make it apparent that he was no more obliged to live by the toil of his brain, than by the sweat of his brow. The same changes in society which rendered it no longer possible for this class of men to pass their lives in idleness have completely put an end to this barbarous pride. It is as obsolete as the fashion of long finger- nails, which in some parts of the East are still the distinctive mark of those who labour not with their hands. All classes are now brought within the reach of your current literature, that literature which, like a moral atmosphere, is as it were the medium of intellectual life, and on the quality of which, according as it may be salubrious or noxious, the health of the public mind depends. There is, if not a general desire for knowledge, a general appearance of such a desire. Authors of all kinds have increased and are increasing among you. Romancers -

Montesinos.—Some of whom attempt things which had hitherto been unattempted yet in prose or rhyme, because among all the extravagant intellects with which the world has teemed none were ever before so utterly extravagant as to choose for themselves themes of such revolting monstrosity.

Sir Thomas More.—Poets -

Montesinos. -

"Tanti Rome non ha preti, o dottori
Bologna."

Sir Thomas More.—Critics -

Montesinos.—More numerous yet; for this is a corps in which many who are destined for better things engage, till they are ashamed of the service; and a much greater number who endeavour to distinguish themselves in higher walks of literature, and fail, take shelter in it; as they cannot attain reputation themselves they endeavour to prevent others from being more successful, and find in the gratification of envy some recompense for disappointed vanity.

Sir Thomas More.—Philosophers -

Montesinos.—True and false; the philosophers and the philosophists; some of the former so full, that it would require, as the rabbis say of a certain pedigree in the Book of Chronicles, four hundred camel loads of commentaries to expound the difficulties in their text; others so empty, that nothing can approximate so nearly to the notion of an infinitesimal quantity as their meaning.

Sir Thomas More.—With this multiplication of books, which in its proportionate increase marvellously exceeds that of your growing population, are you a wiser, a more intellectual, or more imaginative people than when, as in my days, the man of learning, while he sat at his desk, had his whole library within arm's-length?

Montesinos.—If we are not wiser, it must be because the means of knowledge, which are now both abundant and accessible, are either neglected or misused.

The sciences are not here to be considered: in these our progress has been so great, that seeing the moral and religious improvement of the nation has in no degree kept pace with it, you have reasonably questioned whether we have not advanced in certain branches, farther and faster than is conducive to, or perhaps consistent with, the general good. But there can be no question that great advancement has been made in many departments of literature conducive to innocent recreation (which would be alone no trifling good, even were it not, as it is, itself conducive to health both of body and of mind), to sound knowledge, and to moral and political improvement. There are now few portions of the habitable earth which have not been explored, and with a zeal and perseverance which had slept from the first age of maritime discovery till it was revived under George III. in consequence of this revival, and the awakened spirit of curiosity and enterprise, every year adds to our ample store of books relating to the manners of other nations, and the condition of men in states and stages of society different to our own. And of such books we cannot have too many; the idlest reader may find amusement in them of a more satisfactory kind than he can gather from the novel of the day or the criticism of the day; and there are few among them so entirely worthless that the most studious man may not derive from them some information for which he ought to be thankful. Some memorable instances we have had in this generation of the absurdities and errors, sometimes affecting seriously the public service and the national character, which have arisen from the want of such knowledge as by means of such books is now generally diffused. Skates and warming-pans will not again be sent out as ventures to Brazil. The Board of Admiralty will never again attempt to ruin an enemy's port by sinking a stone-ship, to the great amusement of that enemy, in a tide harbour. Nor will a cabinet minister think it sufficient excuse for himself and his colleagues, to confess that they were no better informed than other people, and had everything to learn concerning the interior of a country into which they had sent an army.

Sir Thomas More.—This is but a prospective benefit; and of a humble kind, if it extend no further than to save you from any future exposure of an ignorance which might deserve to be called disgraceful. We profited more by our knowledge of other countries in the age when

"Hops and turkeys, carp and beer,
Came into England all in one year."

Montesinos.—And yet in that age you profited slowly by the commodities which the eastern and western parts of the world afforded. Gold, pearls, and spices were your first imports. For the honour of science and of humanity, medicinal plants were soon sought for. But two centuries elapsed before tea and potatoes—the most valuable products of the East and West—which have contributed far more to the general good than all their spices and gems and precious metals—came into common use; nor have they yet been generally adopted on the Continent, while tobacco found its way to Europe a hundred years earlier; and its filthy abuse, though here happily less than in former times, prevails everywhere.

Sir Thomas More.—Pro pudor! There is a snuff-box on the mantelpiece—and thou revilest tobacco!

Montesinos.—Distinguish, I pray you, gentle ghost! I condemn the abuse of tobacco as filthy, implying in those words that it has its allowable and proper use. To smoke, is, in certain circumstances, a wholesome practice; it may be regarded with a moral complacency as the poor man's luxury, and with liking by any one who follows a lighted pipe in the open air. But whatever may be pleaded for its soothing and intellectualising effects, the odour within doors of a defunct pipe is such an abomination, that I join in anathematising it with James, the best-natured of kings, and Joshua Sylvester, the most voluble of poets.

Sir Thomas More.—Thou hast written verses praise of snuff!

Montesinos.—And if thy nose, sir Spirit, were anything more than the ghost of an olfactor, I would offer it a propitiatory pinch, that you might the more feelingly understand the merit of the said verses, and admire them accordingly. But I am no more to be deemed a snuff-taker because I carry a snuff-box when travelling, and keep one at hand for occasional use, than I am to be reckoned a casuist or a pupil of the Jesuits because the "Moral Philosophy" of Escobar and the "Spiritual Exercises" of St. Ignatius Loyola are on my shelves. Thank Heaven, I bear about with me no habits which I cannot lay aside as easily as my clothes.

The age is past in which travellers could add much to the improvement, the comfort, or the embellishment of this country by imparting anything which they have newly observed in foreign parts. We have happily more to communicate now than to receive. Yet when I tell you that since the commencement of the present century there have been every year, upon an average, more than a hundred and fifty plants which were previously unknown here introduced into the nurseries and market-gardens about London, you will acknowledge that in this branch at least, a constant desire is shown of enriching ourselves with the produce of other hands.

Sir Thomas More.—Philosophers of old travelled to observe the manners of men and study their institutions. I know not whether they found more pleasure in the study, or derived more advantages from it, than the adventurers reap who, in these latter times, have crossed the seas and exposed themselves to dangers of every kind, for the purpose of extending the catalogue of plants.

Montesinos.—Of all travels, those of the mere botanist are the least instructive -

Sir Thomas More.—To any but botanists—but for them alone they are written. Do not depreciate any pursuit which leads men to contemplate the works of their Creator! The Linnean traveller who, when you look over the pages of his journal, seems to you a mere botanist, has in his pursuit, as you have in yours, an object that occupies his time, and fills his mind, and satisfies his heart. It is as innocent as yours, and as disinterested—perhaps more so, because it is not so ambitious. Nor is the pleasure which he partakes in investigating the structure of a plant less pure, or less worthy, than what you derive from perusing the noblest productions of human genius. You look at me as if you thought this reprehension were undeserved!

Montesinos.—The eye, then, Sir Thomas, is proditorious, and I will not gainsay its honest testimony: yet would I rather endeavour to profit by the reprehension than seek to show that it was uncalled for. If I know myself I am never prone to undervalue either the advantages or acquirements which I do not possess. That knowledge is said to be of all others the most difficult; whether it be the most useful the Greeks themselves differ, for if one of their wise men left the words [Greek text which cannot be reproduced] as his maxim to posterity, a poet, who perhaps may have been not less deserving of the title, has controverted it, and told us that for the uses of the world it is more advantageous for us to understand the character of others than to know ourselves.

Sir Thomas More.—Here lies the truth; he who best understands himself is least likely to be deceived in others; you judge of others by yourselves, and therefore measure them by an erroneous standard whenever your autometry is false. This is one reason why the empty critic is usually contumelious and flippant, the competent one as generally equitable and humane.

Montesinos.—This justice I would render to the Linnean school, that it produced our first devoted travellers; the race to which they succeeded employed themselves chiefly in visiting museums and cataloguing pictures, and now and then copying inscriptions; even in their books notices are found for which they who follow them may be thankful; and facts are sometimes, as if by accident, preserved, for useful application. They went abroad to accomplish or to amuse themselves—to improve their time, or to get rid of it; the botanists travelled for the sake of their favourite science, and many of them, in the prime of life, fell victims to their ardour in the unwholesome climates to which they were led. Latterly we have seen this ardour united with the highest genius, the most comprehensive knowledge, and the rarest qualities of perseverance, prudence, and enduring patience. This generation will not leave behind it two names more entitled to the admiration of after ages than Burckhardt and Humboldt. The former purchased this pre- eminence at the cost of his life; the latter lives, and long may he live to enjoy it.

Sir Thomas More.—This very important branch of literature can scarcely be said to have existed in my time; the press was then too much occupied in preserving such precious remains of antiquity as could be rescued from destruction, and in matters which inflamed the minds of men, as indeed they concerned their dearest and most momentous interests. Moreover reviving literature took the natural course of imitation, and the ancients had left nothing in this kind to be imitated. Nothing therefore appeared in it, except the first inestimable relations of the discoveries in the East and West, and these belong rather to the department of history. As travels we had only the chance notices which occurred in the Latin correspondence of learned men when their letters found their way to the public.

Montesinos.—Precious remains these are, but all too few. The first travellers whose journals or memoirs have been preserved were ambassadors; then came the adventurer of whom you speak; and it is remarkable that two centuries afterwards we should find men of the same stamp among the buccaneers, who recorded in like manner with faithful dilligence whatever they had opportunity of observing in their wild and nefarious course of life.

Sir Thomas More.—You may deduce from thence two conclusions, apparently contrarient, yet both warranted by the fact which you have noticed. It may be presumed that men who, while engaged in such an occupation, could thus meritoriously employ their leisure, were rather compelled by disastrous circumstances to such a course than engaged in it by inclination: that it was their misfortune rather than their fault if they were not the benefactors and ornaments of society, instead of being its outlaws; and that under a wise and parental government such persons never would be lost. This is a charitable consideration, nor will I attempt to impugn it; the other may seem less so, but is of more practical importance. For these examples are proof, if proof were needed, that intellectual attainments and habits are no security for good conduct unless they are supported by religious principles; without religion the highest endowments of intellect can only render the possessor more dangerous if he be ill disposed, if well disposed only more unhappy.

The conquerors, as they called themselves, were followed by missionaries.

Montesinos.—Our knowledge of the remoter parts of the world, during the first part of the seventeenth century, must chiefly be obtained from their recitals. And there is no difficulty in separating what may be believed from their fables, because their falsehoods being systematically devised and circulated in pursuance of what they regarded as part of their professional duty, they told truth when they had no motive for deceiving the reader. Let any person compare the relations of our Protestant missionaries with those of the Jesuits, Dominicans, Franciscans, or any other Romish order, and the difference which he cannot fail to perceive between the plain truth of the one and the audacious and elaborate mendacity of the other may lead him to a just inference concerning the two churches.

Sir Thomas More.—Their fables were designed, by exciting admiration, to call forth money for the support of missions, which, notwithstanding such false pretences, were piously undertaken and heroically pursued. They scrupled therefore as little at interlarding their chronicles and annual letters with such miracles, as poets at the use of machinery in their verses. Think not that I am excusing them; but thus it was that they justified their system of imposition to themselves, and this part of it must not be condemned as if it proceeded from an evil intention.

Montesinos.—Yet, Sir Thomas, the best of those missionaries are not more to be admired for their exemplary virtue, and pitied for the superstition which debased their faith, than others of their respective orders are to be abominated for the deliberate wickedness with which, in pursuance of the same system, they imposed the most blasphemous and atrocious legends upon the credulous, and persecuted with fire and sword those who opposed their deceitful villainy. One reason wherefore so few travels were written in the age of which we are speaking is, that no Englishman, unless he were a Papist, could venture into Italy, or any other country where the Romish religion was established in full power, without the danger of being seized by the Inquisition!

Other dangers, by sea and by land, from corsairs and banditti, including too the chances of war and of pestilence, were so great in that age, that it was not unusual for men when they set out upon their travels to put out a sum upon their own lives, which if they died upon the journey was to be the underwriter's gain, but to be repaid if they returned, within such increase as might cover their intervening expenses. The chances against them seem to have been considered as nearly three to one. But danger, within a certain degree, is more likely to provoke adventurers than to deter them.

Sir Thomas More.—There thou hast uttered a comprehensive truth. No legislator has yet so graduated his scale of punishment as to ascertain that degree which shall neither encourage hope nor excite the audacity of desperate guilt. It is certain that there are states of mind in which the consciousness that he is about to play for life or death stimulates a gamester to the throw. This will apply to most of those crimes which are committed for cupidity, and not attended with violence.

Montesinos.—Well then may these hazards have acted as incentives where there was the desire of honour, the spirit of generous enterprise, or even the love of notoriety. By the first of these motives Pietro della Valle (the most romantic in his adventures of all true travellers) was led abroad, the latter spring set in motion my comical countryman, Tom Coriat, who by the engraver's help has represented himself at one time in full dress, making a leg to a courtesan at

Venice, and at another dropping from his rags the all- too lively proofs of prolific poverty.

Perhaps literature has never been so directly benefited by the spirit of trade as it was in the seventeenth century, when European jewellers found their most liberal customers in the courts of the East. Some of the best travels which we possess, as well as the best materials for Persian and Indian history, have been left us by persons engaged in that trade. From that time travelling became less dangerous and more frequent in every generation, except during the late years when Englishmen were excluded from the Continent by the military tyrant whom (with God's blessing on a rightful cause) we have beaten from his imperial throne. And now it is more customary for females in the middle rank of life to visit Italy than it was for them in your days to move twenty miles from home.

Sir Thomas More.—Is this a salutary or an injurious fashion?

Montesinos.—According to the subject, and to the old school maxim quicquid recipitur, recipitur in modum recipientis. The wise come back wiser, the well-informed with richer stores of knowledge, the empty and the vain return as they went, and there are some who bring home foreign vanities and vices in addition to their own.

Sir Thomas More.—And what has been imported by such travellers for the good of their country?

Montesinos.—Coffee in the seventeenth century, inoculation in that which followed; since which we have had now and then a new dance and a new game at cards, curry and mullagatawny soup from the East Indies, turtle from the West, and that earthly nectar to which the East contributes its arrack, and the West its limes and its rum. In the language of men it is called Punch; I know not what may be its name in the Olympian speech. But tell not the Englishmen of George the Second's age, lest they should be troubled for the degeneracy of their grandchildren, that the punchbowl is now become a relic of antiquity, and their beloved beverage almost as obsolete as metheglin, hippocras, chary, or morat!

Sir Thomas More.—It is well for thee that thou art not a young beagle instead of a grey-headed bookman, or that rambling vein of thine would often bring thee under the lash of the whipper-in! Off thou art and away in pursuit of the smallest game that rises before thee.

Montesinos.—Good Ghost, there was once a wise Lord Chancellor, who in a dialogue upon weighty matters thought it not unbecoming to amuse himself with discursive merriment concerning St. Appollonia and St. Uncumber.

Sir Thomas More.—Good Flesh and Blood, that was a nipping reply! And happy man is his dole who retains in grave years, and even to grey hairs, enough of green youth's redundant spirits for such excursiveness! He who never relaxes into sportiveness is a wearisome companion, but beware of him who jests at everything! Such men disparage by some ludicrous association all objects which are presented to their thoughts, and thereby render themselves incapable of any emotion which can either elevate or soften them, they bring upon their moral being an influence more withering than the blast of the desert. A countenance, if it be wrinkled either with smiles or with frowns, is to be shunned; the furrows which the latter leave show that the soil is sour, those of the former are symptomatic of a hollow heart.

None of your travellers have reached Utopia, and brought from thence a fuller account of its institutions?

Montesinos.—There was one, methinks, who must have had it in view when he walked over the world to discover the source of moral motion. He was afflicted with a tympany of mind produced by metaphysics, which was at that time a common complaint, though attended in him with unusual symptoms, but his heart was healthy and strong, and might in former ages have enabled him to acquire a distinguished place among the saints of the Thebais or the philosophers of Greece.

But although we have now no travellers employed in seeking undiscoverable countries, and although Eldorado, the city of the Cesares, and the Sabbatical River, are expunged even from the maps of credulity and imagination, Welshmen have gone in search of Madoc's descendants, and scarcely a year passes without adding to the melancholy list of those who have perished in exploring the interior of Africa.

Sir Thomas More.—Whenever there shall exist a civilised and Christian negro state Providence will open that country to civilisation and Christianity, meantime to risk strength and enterprise and science against climate is contending against the course of nature. Have these travellers yet obtained for you the secret of the Psylli?

Montesinos.—We have learnt from savages the mode of preparing their deadliest poisons. The more useful knowledge by which they render the human body proof against the most venomous serpents has not been sought with equal diligence; there are, however, scattered notices which may perhaps afford some clue to the discovery. The writings of travellers are not more rich in materials for the poet and the historian than they are in useful notices, deposited there like seeds which lie deep in the earth till some chance brings them within reach of air, and then they germinate. These are fields in which something may always be found by the gleaner, and therefore those general collections in which the works are curtailed would be to be reprobated, even if epitomisers did not seem to possess a certain instinct of generic doltishness which leads them curiously to omit whatever ought especially to be preserved.

Sir Thomas More.—If ever there come a time, Montesinos, when beneficence shall be as intelligent, and wisdom as active, as the spirit of trade, you will then draw from foreign countries other things beside those which now pay duties at the custom-house, or are cultivated in nurseries for the conservatories of the wealthy. Not that I regard with dissatisfaction these latter importations of luxury, however far they may be brought, or at whatever cost; for of all mere pleasures those of a garden are the most salutary, and approach nearest to a moral enjoyment. But you will then (should that time come) seek and find in the laws, usages and experience of other nations palliatives for some of those evils and diseases which have hitherto been inseparable from society and human nature, and remedies, perhaps, for others.

Montesinos.—Happy the travellers who shall be found instrumental to such good! One advantage belongs to authors of this description; because they contribute to the instruction of the learned, their reputation suffers no diminution by the course of time: age rather enhances their value. In this respect they resemble historians, to whom, indeed, their labours are in a great degree subsidiary.

Sir Thomas More.—They have an advantage over them, my friend, in this, that rarely can they leave evil works behind them, which either from a mischievous persuasion, or a malignant purpose, may heap condemnation upon their own souls as long as such works survive them. Even if they should manifest pernicious opinions and a wicked will, the venom is in a great degree sheathed by the vehicle in which it is administered. And this is something; for let me tell thee, thou consumer of goose quills, that of all the Devil's laboratories there is none in which more poison is concocted for mankind than in the inkstand!

Montesinos.—"My withers are unwrung!"

Sir Thomas More.—Be thankful, therefore, in life, as thou wilt in death.

A principle of compensation may be observed in literary pursuits as in other things. Reputations that never flame continue to glimmer for centuries after those which blaze highest have gone out. And what is of more moment, the humblest occupations are morally the safest. Rhadamanthus never puts on his black cap to pronounce sentence upon a dictionary-maker or the compiler of a county history.

Montesinos. I am to understand, then, that in the archangel's balance a little book may sink the scale toward the pit; while all the tomes of Thomas Hearne and good old John Nichols will be weighed among their good works!

Sir Thomas More.—Sport as thou wilt in allusions to allegory and fable; but bear always in thy most serious mind this truth, that men hold under an awful responsibility the talents with which they are entrusted. Kings have not so serious an account to render as they who exercise an intellectual influence over the minds of men!

Montesinos.—If evil works, so long as they continue to produce evil, heap up condemnation upon the authors, it is well for some of the wickedest writers that their works do not survive them.

Sir Thomas More.—Such men, my friend, even by the most perishable of their wicked works, lay up sufficient condemnation for themselves. The maxim that malitia supplet aetatem is rightfully admitted in human laws: should there not then, by parity of justice, be cases where, when the secrets of the heart are seen, the intention shall be regarded rather than the act?

The greatest portion of your literature, at any given time, is ephemeral; indeed, it has ever been so since the discovery of printing; and this portion it is which is most influential, consequently that by which most good or mischief is done.

Montesinos.—Ephemeral it truly may be called; it is now looked for by the public as regularly as their food; and, like food, it affects the recipient surely and permanently, even when its effect is slow, according as it is wholesome or noxious. But how great is the difference between the current literature of this and of any former time!

Sir Thomas More.—From that complacent tone it may be presumed that you see in it proof both of moral and intellectual improvement. Montesinos, I must disturb that comfortable opinion, and call upon you to examine how much of this refinement which passes for improvement is superficial. True it is that controversy is carried on with more decency than it was by Martin Lutherand a certain Lord Chancellor, to whom you just now alluded; but if more courtesy is to be found in polemical writers, who are less sincere than either the one or the other, there is as much acerbity of feeling and as much bitterness of heart. You have a class of miscreants which had no existence in those days—the panders of the press, who live by administering to the vilest passions of the people, and encouraging their most dangerous errors, practising upon their ignorance, and inculcating whatever is most pernicious in principle and most dangerous to society. This is their golden age; for though such men would in any age have taken to some villainy or other, never could they have found a course at once so gainful and so safe. Long impunity has taught them to despise the laws which they defy, and the institutions which they are labouring to subvert; any further responsibility enters not into their creed, if that may be called a creed, in which all the articles are negative. I? we turn from politics to what should be humaner literature, and look at the self- constituted censors of whatever has passed the press, there also we shall find that they who are the most incompetent assume the most authority, and that the public favour such pretensions; for in quackery of every kind, whether medical, political, critical, or hypocritical, quo quis impudentior eo doctior habetur.

Montesinos.—The pleasure which men take in acting maliciously is properly called by Barrow a RASCALLY delight. But this is no new form of malice. "Avant nous," says the sagacious but iron-hearted Montluc—"avant nous ces envies ont regne, et regneront encore apres nous, si Dieu ne nous voulait tous refondre." Its worst effect is that which Ben Jonson remarked: "The gentle reader," says he, "rests happy to hear the worthiest works misrepresented, the clearest actions obscured, the innocentest life traduced; and in such a licence of lying, a field so fruitful of slanders, how can there be matter wanting to his laughter? Hence comes the epidemical infection: for how can they escape the contagion of the writings whom the virulency of the calumnies hath not staved off from reading?"

There is another mischief, arising out of ephemeral literature, which was noticed by the same great author. "Wheresoever manners and fashions are corrupted," says he, "language is. It imitates the public riot. The excess of feasts and apparel are the notes of a sick state; and the wantonness of language of a sick mind." This was the observation of a man well versed in the history of the ancients and in their literature. The evil prevailed in his time to a considerable degree; but it was not permanent, because it proceeded rather from the affectation of a few individuals than from any general cause: the great poets were free from it; and our prose writers then, and till the end of that century, were preserved, by their sound studies and logical habits of mind, from any of those faults into which men fall who write loosely because they think loosely. The pedantry of one class and the colloquial vulgarity of another had their day; the faults of each were strongly contrasted, and better writers kept the mean between them. More lasting effect was produced by translators, who in later times have corrupted our idiom as much as, in early ones, they enriched our vocabulary; and to this injury the Scotch have greatly contributed; for composing in a language which is not their mother tongue, they necessarily acquired an artificial and formal style, which, not so much through the merit of a few as owing to the perseverance of others, who for half a century seated themselves on the bench of criticism, has almost superseded the vernacular English of Addison and Swift. Our journals, indeed, have been the great corrupters of our style, and continue to be so, and not for this reason only. Men who write in newspapers, and magazines, and reviews, write for present effect; in most cases this is as much their natural and proper aim as it would be in public speaking; but when it is so they consider, like public speakers, not so much what is accurate or just, either in matter or manner, as what will be acceptable to those whom they address. Writing also under the excitement of emulation and rivalry, they seek, by all the artifices and efforts of an ambitious style, to dazzle their readers; and they are wise in their generation, experience having shown that common minds are taken by glittering faults, both in prose and verse, as larks are with looking-glasses.

In this school it is that most writers are now trained; and after such training anything like an easy and natural movement is as little to be looked for in their compositions as in the step of a dancing master. To the vices of style which are thus generated there must be added the inaccuracies inevitably arising from haste, when a certain quantity of matter is to be supplied for a daily or weekly publication which allows of no delay—the slovenliness that confidence, as well as fatigue and inattention, will produce—and the barbarisms, which are the effect of ignorance, or that smattering of knowledge which serves only to render ignorance presumptuous. These are the causes of corruption in our current style; and when these are considered there would be ground for apprehending that the best writings of the last century might become as obsolete as yours in the like process of time, if we had not in our Liturgy and our Bible a standard from which it will not be possible wholly to depart.

Sir Thomas More.—Will the Liturgy and the Bible keep the language at that standard in the colonies, where little or no use is made of the one, and not much, it may be feared, of the other?

Montesinos.—A sort of hybrid speech, a Lingua Anglica, more debased, perhaps, than the Lingua Franca of the Levant, or the Portuguese of Malabar, is likely enough to grow up among the South Sea Islands; like the mixture of Spanish with some of the native languages in South America, or the mingle-mangle which the negroes have made with French and English, and probably with other European tongues in the colonies of their respective states. The spirit of mercantile adventure may produce in this part of the new world a process analogous to what took place throughout Europe on the breaking up of the Western Empire; and in the next millennium these derivatives may become so many cultivated tongues, having each its literature. These will be like varieties in a flower-garden, which the florist raises from seed; but in the colonies, as in our orchards, the graft takes with it, and will preserve, the true characteristics of the stock.

Sir Thomas More.—But the same causes of deterioration will be at work there also.

Montesinos.—Not nearly in the same degree, nor to an equal extent. Now and then a word with the American impress comes over to us which has not been struck in the mint of analogy. But the Americans are more likely to be infected by the corruption of our written language than we are to have it debased by any importations of this kind from them.

Sir Thomas More.—There is a more important consideration belonging to this subject. The cause which you have noticed as the principal one of this corruption must have a farther and more mischievous effect. For it is not in the vices of an ambitious style that these ephemeral writers, who live upon the breath of popular applause, will rest. Great and lasting reputations, both in ancient and modern times, have been raised notwithstanding that defect, when the ambition from which it proceeded was of a worthy kind, and was sustained by great powers and adequate acquirements. But this ambition, which looks beyond the morrow, has no place in the writers of a day. Present effect is their end and aim; and too many of them, especially the ablest, who have wanted only moral worth to make them capable of better things, are persons who can "desire no other mercy from after ages than silence and oblivion." Even with the better part of the public that author will always obtain the most favourable reception, who keeps most upon a level with them in intellectuals, and puts them to the least trouble of thinking. He who addresses himself with the whole endeavours of a powerful mind to the understanding faculty may find fit readers; but they will be few. He who labours for posterity in the fields of research, must look to posterity for his reward. Nay, even they whose business is with the feelings and the fancy, catch most fish when they angle in shallow waters. Is it not so, Piscator?

Montesinos.—In such honest anglers, Sir Thomas, I should look for as many virtues, as good old happy Izaak Walton found in his brethren of the rod and line. Nor will you, I think, disparage them; for you were of the Rhymers' Company, and at a time when things appear to us in their true colours and proportion (if ever while we are yet in the body), you remembered your verses with more satisfaction than your controversial writings, even though you had no misgivings concerning the part which you had chosen.

Sir Thomas More.—My verses, friend, had none of the athanasia in their composition. Though they have not yet perished, they cannot be said to have a living existence; even you, I suspect, have sought for them rather because of our personal acquaintance than for any other motive. Had I been only a poet, those poems, such as they were, would have preserved my name; but being remembered for other grounds, better and worse, the name which I have left has been one cause why they have passed into oblivion, sooner than their perishable nature would have carried them thither. If in the latter part of my mortal existence I had misgivings concerning any of my writings, they were of the single one, which is still a living work, and which will continue so to be. I feared that speculative opinions, which had been intended for the possible but remote benefit of mankind, might, by unhappy circumstances, be rendered instrumental to great and immediate evil; an apprehension, however, which was altogether free from self-reproach.

But my verses will continue to exist in their mummy state, long after the worms shall have consumed many of those poetical reputations which are at this time in the cherry-cheeked bloom of health and youth. Old poets will always retain their value for antiquaries and philologists, modern ones are far too numerous ever to acquire an accidental usefulness of this kind, even if the language were to undergo greater changes than any circumstances are likely to produce. There will now be more poets in every generation than in that which preceded it; they will increase faster than your population; and as their number increases, so must the proportion of those who will be remembered necessarily diminish. Tell the Fitz- Muses this! It is a consideration, Sir Poet, which may serve as a refrigerant for their ardour. Those of the tribe who may flourish hereafter (as the flourishing phrase is) in any particular age, will be little more remembered in the next than the Lord Mayors and Sheriffs who were their contemporaries.

Montesinos.—Father in verse, if you had not put off flesh and blood so long, you would not imagine that this consideration will diminish their number. I am sure it would not have affected me forty years ago, had I seen this truth then as clearly as I perceive and feel it now. Though it were manifest to all men that not one poet in an age, in a century, a millennium, could establish his claim to be for ever known, every aspirant would persuade himself that he is the happy person for whom the inheritance of fame is reserved. And when the dream of immortality is dispersed, motives enough remain for reasonable ambition.

It is related of some good man (I forget who), that upon his death- bed he recommended his son to employ himself in cultivating a garden, and in composing verses, thinking these to be at once the happiest and the most harmless of all pursuits. Poetry may be, and too often has been, wickedly perverted to evil purposes; what indeed is there that may not, when religion itself is not safe from such abuses! but the good which it does inestimably exceeds the evil. It is no trifling good to provide means of innocent and intellectual enjoyment for so many thousands in a state like ours; an enjoyment, heightened, as in every instance it is within some little circle, by personal considerations, raising it to a degree which may deserve to be called happiness. It is no trifling good to win the ear of children with verses which foster in them the seeds of humanity and tenderness and piety, awaken their fancy, and exercise pleasurably and wholesomely their imaginative and meditative powers. It is no trifling benefit to provide a ready mirror for the young, in which they may see their own best feelings reflected, and wherein "whatsoever things are honest, whatsoever things are just, whatsoever things are pure, whatsoever things are lovely," are presented to them in the most attractive form. It is no trifling benefit to send abroad strains which may assist in preparing the heart for its trials, and in supporting it under them. But there is a greater good than this, a farther benefit. Although it is in verse that the most consummate skill in composition is to be looked for, and all the artifice of language displayed, yet it is in verse only that we throw off the yoke of the world, and are as it were privileged to utter our deepest and holiest feelings. Poetry in this respect may be called the salt of the earth; we express in it, and receive in it, sentiments for which, were it not for this permitted medium, the usages of the world would neither allow utterance nor acceptance. And who can tell in our heart-chilling and heart-hardening society, how much more selfish, how much more debased, how much worse we should have been, in all moral and intellectual respects, had it not been for the unnoticed and unsuspected influence of this preservative? Even much of that poetry, which is in its composition worthless, or absolutely bad, contributes to this good.

Sir Thomas More.—Such poetry, then, according to your view, is to be regarded with indulgence.

Montesinos.—Thank Heaven, Sir Thomas, I am no farther critical than every author must necessarily be who makes a careful study of his own art. To understand the principles of criticism is one thing; to be what is called critical, is another; the first is like being versed in jurisprudence, the other like being litigious. Even those poets who contribute to the mere amusement of their readers, while that amusement is harmless, are to be regarded with complacency, if not respect. They are the butterflies of literature, who during the short season of their summer, enliven the garden and the field. It were pity to touch them even with a tender hand, lest we should brush the down from their wings.

Sir Thomas More.—These are they of whom I spake as angling in shallow waters. You will not regard with the same complacency those who trouble the stream; still less those who poison it.

Montesinos.—"Vesanum tetigisse timent, fugiuntque poetam Qui sapiunt; agitant pueri, incautique sequuntur."

Sir Thomas More.—This brings us again to the point at which you bolted. The desire of producing present effect, the craving for immediate reputation, have led to another vice, analogous to and connected with that of the vicious style, which the same causes are producing, but of worse consequences. The corruption extends from the manner to the matter; and they who brew for the press, like some of those who brew for the publicans, care not, if the potion has but its desired strength, how deleterious may be the ingredients which they use. Horrors at which the innocent heart quails, and the healthy stomachs heaves in loathing, are among the least hurtful of their stimulants.

Montesinos.—This too, Sir Thomas, is no new evil. An appetite for horrors is one of the diseased cravings of the human mind; and in old times the tragedies which most abounded in them, were for that reason the most popular. The dramatists of our best age, great Ben and greater Shakespeare excepted, were guilty of a farther sin, with which the writers whom you censure are also to be reproached; they excited their auditors by the representation of monstrous crimes— crimes out of the course of nature. Such fables might lawfully be brought upon the Grecian stage, because the belief of the people divested them of their odious and dangerous character; there they were well known stories, regarded with a religious persuasion of their truth; and the personages, being represented as under the overruling influence of dreadful destiny, were regarded therefore with solemn commiseration, not as voluntary and guilty agents. There is nothing of this to palliate or excuse the production of such stories in later times; the choice, and, in a still greater degree, the invention of any such, implies in the author, not merely a want of judgment, but a defect in moral feeling. Here, however, the dramatists of that age stopped. They desired to excite in their audience the pleasure of horror, and this was an abuse of the poet's art: but they never aimed at disturbing their moral perceptions, at presenting wickedness in an attractive form, exciting sympathy with guilt, and admiration for villainy, thereby confounding the distinctions between right and wrong. This has been done in our days; and it has accorded so well with the tendency of other things, that the moral drift of a book is no longer regarded, and the severest censure which can be passed upon it is to say that it is in bad taste; such is the phrase— and the phrase is not confined to books alone. Anything may be written, said, or done, in bad feeling and with a wicked intent; and the public are so tolerant of these, that he who should express a displeasure on that score would be censured for bad taste himself!

Sir Thomas More.—And yet you talked of the improvement of the age, and of the current literature as exceeding in worth that of any former time

Montesinos.—The portion of it which shall reach to future times will justify me; for we have living minds who have done their duty to their own age and to posterity.

Sir Thomas More.—Has the age in return done its duty to them?

Montesinos.—They complain not of the age, but they complain of an anomalous injustice in the laws. They complain that authors are deprived of a perpetual property in the produce of their own labours, when all other persons enjoy it as an indefeasible and acknowledged right. And they ask upon what principle, with what equity, or under what pretence of public good they are subjected to this injurious enactment? Is it because their labour is so light, the endowments which are required for it so common, the attainments so cheaply and easily acquired, and the present remuneration in all cases so adequate, so ample, and so certain?

The act whereby authors are deprived of that property in their own works which, upon every principle of reason, natural justice, and common law, they ought to enjoy, is so curiously injurious in its operation, that it bears with most hardship upon the best works. For books of great immediate popularity have their run and come to a dead stop: the hardship is upon those which win their way slowly and difficultly, but keep the field at last. And it will not appear surprising that this should generally have been the case with books of the highest merit, if we consider what obstacles to the success of a work may be opposed by the circumstances and obscurity of the author, when he presents himself as a candidate for fame, by the humour or the fashion of the times; the taste of the public, more likely to be erroneous than right at any time; and the incompetence, or personal malevolence of some unprincipled critic, who may take upon himself to guide the public opinion, and who if he feels in his own heart that the fame of the man whom he hates is invulnerable, lays in wait for that reason the more vigilantly to wound him in his fortunes. In such cases, when the copyright as by the existing law departs from the author's family at his death, or at the end of twenty-eight years from the first publication of every work, (if he dies before the expiration of that term,) his representatives are deprived of their property just as it would begin to prove a valuable inheritance.

The last descendants of Milton died in poverty. The descendants of Shakespeare are living in poverty, and in the lowest condition of life. Is this just to these individuals? Is it grateful to the memory of those who are the pride and boast of their country? Is it honourable, or becoming to us as a nation, holding—the better part of us assuredly, and the majority affecting to hold—the names of Shakespeare and Milton in veneration?

To have placed the descendants of Shakespeare and Milton in respectability and comfort—in that sphere of life where, with a full provision for our natural wants and social enjoyments, free scope is given to the growth of our intellectual and immortal part, simple justice was all that was required, only that they should have possessed the perpetual copyright of their ancestors' works, only that they should not have been deprived of their proper inheritance.

The decision which time pronounces upon the reputation of authors, and upon the permanent rank which they are to hold in the estimation of posterity, is unerring and final. Restore to them that perpetuity in the property of their works, of which the law has deprived them, and the reward of literary labour will ultimately be in just proportion to its deserts.

However slight may be the hope of obtaining any speedy redress, there is some satisfaction in earnestly protesting against this injustice. And believing as I do, that if society continues to improve, no injustice will long be permitted to continue after it has been fairly exposed, and is clearly apprehended, I cannot but believe that a time must come when the rights of literature will be acknowledged and its wrongs redressed; and that those authors hereafter who shall deserve well of posterity, will have no cause to reproach themselves for having sacrificed the interests of their children when they disregarded the pursuit of fortune for themselves.

COLLOQUY VII

THE CONCLUSION

MONTESINOS.—Here Sir Thomas is the opinion which I have attempted to maintain concerning the progress and tendency of society, placed in a proper position, and inexpugnably entrenched here according to the rules of art, by the ablest of all moral engineers.

Sir Thomas More.—Who may this political Achilles be whom you have called in to your assistance?

Montesinos.—Whom Fortune rather has sent to my aid, for my reading has never been in such authors. I have endeavoured always to drink from the spring-head, but never ventured out to fish in deep waters. Thor, himself, when he had hooked the Great Serpent, was unable to draw him up from the abyss.

Sir Thomas More—The waters in which you have now been angling have been shallow enough, if the pamphlet in your hand is, as it appears to be, a magazine.

Montesinos.—"Ego sum is," said Scaliger, "qui ab omnibus discere volo; neque tam malum librum esse puto, ex quo non aliquem fructum colligere possum." I think myself repaid, in a monkish legend, for examining a mass of inane fiction, if I discover a single passage which elucidates the real history or manners of its age. In old poets of the third and fourth order we are contented with a little ore, and a great deal of dross. And so in publications of this kind, prejudicial as they are to taste and public feeling, and the public before deeply injurious to the real interests of literature, something may sometimes be found to compensate for the trash and tinsel and insolent flippancy, which are now become the staple commodities of such journals. This number contains Kant's idea of a Universal History on a Cosmo-Political plan; and that Kant is as profound a philosopher as his disciples have proclaimed him to be, this little treatise would fully convince me, if I had not already believed it, in reliance upon one of the very few men who are capable of forming a judgment upon such a writer.

The sum of his argument is this: that as deaths, births, and marriages, and the oscillations of the weather, irregular as they seem to be in themselves, are nevertheless reduceable upon the great scale to certain rules; so there may be discovered in the course of human history a steady and continuous, though slow development of certain great predispositions in human nature, and that although men neither act under the law of instinct, like brute animals, nor under the law of a preconcerted plan, like rational cosmopolites, the great current of human actions flows in a regular stream of tendency toward this development; individuals and nations, while pursuing their own peculiar and often contradictory purposes, following the guidance of a great natural purpose, and thus promoting a process which, even if they perceived it, they would little regard. What that process is he states in the following series of propositions:-

1st. All tendencies of any creature, to which it is predisposed by nature, are destined in the end to develop themselves perfectly and agreeably to their final purpose.

2nd. In man, as the sole rational creature upon earth, those tendencies which have the use of his reason for their object are destined to obtain their perfect development in the species only, and not in the individual.

3rd. It is the will of nature that man should owe to himself alone everything which transcends the mere mechanic constitution of his animal existence, and that he should be susceptible of no other happiness or perfection than what he has created for himself, instinct apart, through his own reason.

4th. The means which nature employs to bring about the development of all the tendencies she has laid in man, is the antagonism of those tendencies in the social state, no farther, however, than to that point at which this antagonism becomes the cause of social arrangements founded in law.

5th. The highest problem for the human species, to the solution of which it is irresistibly urged by natural impulses, is the establishment of a universal civil society, founded on the empire of political justice.

6th. This problem is, at the same time, the most difficult of all, and the one which is latest solved by man.

7th. The problem of the establishment of a perfect constitution of society depends upon the problem of a system of international relations, adjusted to law, and apart from this latter problem cannot be solved.

8th. The history of the human race, as a whole, may be regarded as the unravelling of a hidden plan of nature for accomplishing a perfect state of civil constitution for society in its internal relations (and as the condition of that, by the last proposition, in its external relations also), as the sole state of society in which the tendencies of human nature can be all and fully developed.

Sir Thomas More.—This is indeed a master of the sentences, upon whose text it may be profitable to dwell. Let us look to his propositions. From the first this conclusion must follow, that as nature has given men all his faculties for use, any system of society in which the moral and intellectual powers of any portion of the people are left undeveloped for want of cultivation, or receive a perverse direction, is plainly opposed to the system of nature, in other words, to the will of God. Is there any government upon earth that will bear this test?

Montesinos.—I should rather ask of you, will there ever be one?

Sir Thomas More.—Not till there be a system of government conducted in strict conformity to the precepts of the Gospel.

Montesinos.

"Offer these truths to Power, will she obey?
It prunes her pomp, perchance ploughs up the root."
LORD BROOKE.

Yet, in conformity to those principles alone, it is that subjects can find their perfect welfare, and States their full security. Christianity may be long in obtaining the victory over the powers of this world, but when that consummation shall have taken place the converse of his second proposition will hold good, for the species having obtained its perfect development, the condition of society must then be such that individuals will obtain it also as a necessary consequence.

Sir Thomas More.—Here you and your philosopher part company. For he asserts that man is left to deduce from his own unassisted reason everything which relates not to his mere material nature.

Montesinos.—There, indeed, I must diverge from him, and what in his language is called the hidden plan of nature, in mine will be the revealed will of God.

Sir Thomas More.—The will is revealed; but the plan is hidden. Let man dutifully obey that will, and the perfection of society and of human nature will be the result of such obedience; but upon obedience they depend. Blessings and curses are set before you—for nations as for individuals—yea, for the human race.

Flatter not yourself with delusive expectations! The end may be according to your hope—whether it will be so (which God grant!) is as inscrutable for angels as for men. But to descry that great struggles are yet to come is within reach of human foresight—that great tribulations must needs accompany them—and that these may be- -you know not how near at hand!

Throughout what is called the Christian world there will be a contest between Impiety and Religion; the former everywhere is gathering strength, and wherever it breaks loose the foundations of human society will be shaken. Do not suppose that you are safe from this danger because you are blest with a pure creed, a reformed ritual, and a tolerant Church! Even here the standard of impiety has been set up; and the drummers who beat the march of intellect through your streets, lanes, and market-places, are enlisted under it.

The struggle between Popery and Protestanism is renewed. And let no man deceive himself by a vain reliance upon the increased knowledge, or improved humanity of the times! Wickedness is ever the same; and you never were in so much danger from moral weakness.

Co-existent with these struggles is that between the feudal system of society as variously modified throughout Europe, and the levelling principle of democracy. That principle is actively and indefatigably at work in these kingdoms, allying itself as occasion may serve with Popery or with Dissent, with atheism or with fanaticism, with profligacy or with hypocrisy, ready confederates, each having its own sinister views, but all acting to one straightforward end. Your rulers meantime seem to be trying that experiment with the British Constitution which Mithridates is said to have tried upon his own; they suffer poison to be administered in daily doses, as if they expected that by such a course the public mind would at length be rendered poison-proof!

The first of these struggles will affect all Christendom; the third may once again shake the monarchies of Europe. The second will be felt widely; but nowhere with more violence than in Ireland, that unhappy country, wherein your government, after the most impolitic measures into which weakness was ever deluded, or pusillanimity intimidated, seems to have abdicated its functions, contenting itself with the semblance of an authority which it has wanted either wisdom or courage to exert.

There is a fourth danger, the growth of your manufacturing system; and this is peculiarly your own. You have a great and increasing population, exposed at all times by the fluctuations of trade to suffer the severest privations in the midst of a rich and luxurious society, under little or no restraint from religious principle, and if not absolutely disaffected to the institutions of the country, certainly not attached to them: a class of men aware of their numbers and of their strength; experienced in all the details of combination; improvident when they are in the receipt of good wages, yet feeling themselves injured when those wages, during some failure of demand, are so lowered as no longer to afford the means of comfortable subsistence; and directing against the government and the laws of the country their resentment and indignation for the evils which have been brought upon them by competition and the spirit of rivalry in trade. They have among them intelligent heads and daring minds; and you have already seen how perilously they may be wrought upon by seditious journalists and seditious orators in a time of distress.

On what do you rely for security against these dangers? On public opinion? You might as well calculate upon the constancy of wind and weather in this uncertain climate. On the progress of knowledge? it is such knowledge as serves only to facilitate the course of delusion. On the laws? the law which should be like a sword in a strong hand, is weak as a bulrush if it be feebly administered in time of danger. On the people? they are divided. On the Parliament? every faction will be fully and formidably represented there. On the government? it suffers itself to be insulted and defied at home, and abroad it has shown itself incapable of maintaining the relations of peace and amity with its allies, so far has it been divested of power by the usurpation of the press. It is at peace with Spain, and it is at peace with Turkey; and although no government was ever more desirous of acting with good faith, its subjects are openly assisting the Greeks with men and money against the one, and the Spanish Americans against the other. Athens, in the most turbulent times of its democracy, was not more effectually domineered over by its demagogues than you are by the press—a press which is not only without restraint, but without responsibility; and in the management of which those men will always have most power who have least probity, and have most completely divested themselves of all sense of honour and all regard for truth.

The root of all your evils is in the sinfulness of the nation. The principle of duty is weakened among you; that of moral obligation is loosened; that of religious obedience is destroyed. Look at the worldliness of all classes—the greediness of the rich, the misery of the poor, and the appalling depravity which is spreading among the lower classes through town and country; a depravity which proceeds unchecked because of the total want of discipline, and for which there is no other corrective than what may be supplied by fanaticism, which is itself an evil.

If there be nothing exaggerated in this representation, you must acknowledge that though the human race, considered upon the great scale, should be proceeding toward the perfectibility for which it may be designed, the present aspects in these kingdoms are nevertheless rather for evil than for good. Sum you up now upon the hopeful side.

Montesinos—First, then. I rest in a humble but firm reliance upon that Providence which sometimes in its mercy educes from the errors of men a happier issue than could ever have been attained by their wisdom;—that Providence which has delivered this nation from so many and such imminent dangers heretofore.

Looking, then, to human causes, there is hope to be derived from the humanising effects of Literature, which has now first begun to act upon all ranks. Good principles are indeed used as the stalking- horse under cover of which pernicious designs may be advanced; but the better seeds are thus disseminated and fructify after the ill design has failed.

The cruelties of the old criminal law have been abrogated. Debtors are no longer indiscriminately punished by indefinite imprisonment. The iniquity of the slave trade has been acknowledged, and put an end to, so far as the power of this country extends; and although slavery is still tolerated, and must be so for awhile, measures have been taken for alleviating it while it continues, and preparing the way for its gradual and safe removal. These are good works of the government. And when I look upon the conduct of that government in all its foreign relations, though there may be some things to disapprove, and some sins of omission to regret, it has been, on the whole, so disinterested, so magnanimous, so just, that this reflection gives me a reasonable and a religious ground of hope. And the reliance is strengthened when I call to mind that missionaries from Great Britain are at this hour employed in spreading the glad tidings of the Gospel far and wide among heathen nations.

Descending from these wider views to the details of society, there, too, I perceive ground, if not for confidence, at least for hope. There is a general desire throughout the higher ranks for bettering the condition of the poor, a subject to which the government also has directed its patient attention: minute inquiries have been made into their existing state, and the increase of pauperism and of crimes. In no other country have the wounds of the commonwealth been so carefully probed. By means of colonisation, of an improved parochial order and of a more efficient police, the further increase of these evils may be prevented; while, by education, by providing means of religious instruction for all by savings banks, and perhaps by the establishment of Owenite communities among themselves, the labouring classes will have their comforts enlarged, and their well- being secured, if they are not wanting to themselves in prudence and good conduct. A beginning has been made—an impulse given: it may be hoped—almost, I will say, it may be expected—that in a few generations this whole class will be placed within the reach of moral and intellectual gratifications, whereby they may be rendered healthier, happier, better in all respects, an improvement which will be not more beneficial to them as individuals, than to the whole body of the commonweal.

The diffusion of literature, though it has rendered the acquirement of general knowledge impossible, and tends inevitably to diminish the number of sound scholars, while it increases the multitude of sciolists, carries with it a beneficial influence to the lower classes. Our booksellers already perceive that it is their interest to provide cheap publications for a wide public, instead of looking to the rich alone as their customers. There is reason to expect that, in proportion as this is done—in proportion as the common people are supplied with wholesome entertainment (and wholesome it is, if it be only harmless) they will be less liable to be acted upon by fanaticism and sedition.

You have not exaggerated the influence of the newspaper press, nor the profligacy of some of those persons, by whom this unrestrained and irresponsible power is exercised. Nevertheless it has done, and is doing, great and essential good. The greatest evils in society proceed from the abuse of power; and this, though abundantly manifested in the newspapers themselves, they prevent in other quarters. No man engaged in public life could venture now upon such transactions as no one, in their station half a century ago, would have been ashamed of. There is an end of that scandalous jobbing which at that time existed in every department of the State, and in every branch of the public service; and a check is imposed upon any scandalous and unfit promotion, civil or ecclesiastical. By whatever persons the government may be administered, they are now well aware that they must do nothing which will not bear daylight and strict investigation. The magistrates also are closely observed by this self-constituted censorship; and the inferior officers cannot escape exposure for any perversion of justice, or undue exercise of authority. Public nuisances are abated by the same means, and public grievances which the Legislature might else overlook, are forced upon its attention. Thus, in ordinary times, the utility of this branch of the press is so great that one of the worst evils to be apprehended from the abuse of its power at all times, and the wicked purposes to which it is directed in dangerous ones, is the ultimate loss of a liberty, which is essential to the public good, but which when it passes into licentiousness, and effects the overthrow of a State, perishes in the ruin it has brought on.

In the fine arts, as well as in literature, a levelling principle is going on, fatal, perhaps, to excellence, but favourable to mediocrity. Such facilities are afforded to imitative talent, that whatever is imitable will be imitated. Genius will often be suppressed by this, and when it exerts itself, will find it far more difficult to obtain notice than in former times. There is the evil here that ingenious persons are seduced into a profession which is already crowded with unfortunate adventurers; but, on the other hand, there is a great increase of individual and domestic enjoyment. Accomplishments which were almost exclusively professional in the last age, are now to be found in every family within a certain rank of life. Wherever there is a disposition for the art of design, it is cultivated, and in consequence of the general proficiency in this most useful of the fine arts, travellers represent to our view the manners and scenery of the countries which they visit, as well by the pencil as the pen. By means of two fortunate discoveries in the art of engraving, these graphic representations are brought within the reach of whole classes who were formerly precluded by the expense of such things from these sources of gratification and instruction. Artists and engravers of great name are now, like authors and booksellers, induced to employ themselves for this lower and wider sphere of purchasers. In all this I see the cause as well as the effect of a progressive refinement, which must be beneficial in many ways. This very diffusion of cheap books and cheap prints may, in its natural consequences, operate rather to diminish than to increase the number of adventurers in literature and in the arts. For though at first it will create employment for greater numbers, yet in another generation imitative talent will become so common, that neither parents nor possessors will mistake it for an indication of extraordinary genius, and many will thus be saved from a ruinous delusion. More pictures will be painted but fewer exhibited, more poetry written but less published, and in both arts talents which might else have been carried to an overstocked and unprofitable market, will be cultivated for their own sakes, and for the gratification of private circles, becoming thus a source of sure enjoyment and indirectly of moral good. Scientific pursuits will, in like manner, be extended, and pursuits which partake of science, and afford pleasures within the reach of humble life.

Here, then, is good in progress which will hold on its course, and the growth of which will only be suspended, not destroyed, during any of those political convulsions which may too probably be apprehended—too probably, I say, because when you call upon me to consider the sinfulness of this nation, my heart fails. There can be no health, no soundness in the state, till government shall regard the moral improvement of the people as its first great duty. The same remedy is required for the rich and for the poor. Religion ought to be so blended with the whole course of instruction, that its doctrines and precepts should indeed "drop as the rain, and distil as the dew, as the small rain upon the tender herb, and as the showers upon the grass"—the young plants would then imbibe it, and the heart and intellect assimilate it with their growth. We are, in a great degree, what our institutions make us. Gracious God were those institutions adapted to Thy will and word—were we but broken in from childhood to Thy easy yoke—were we but carefully instructed to believe and obey—in that obedience and belief we should surely find our temporal welfare and our eternal happiness!

Here, indeed, I tremble at the prospect! Could I look beyond the clouds and the darkness which close upon it, I should then think that there may come a time when that scheme for a perpetual peace among the states of Christendom which Henri IV. formed, and which has been so ably digested by the Abbe St. Pierre, will no longer be regarded as the speculation of a visionary. The Holy Alliance, imperfect and unstable as it is, is in itself a recognition of the principle. At this day it would be practicable, if one part of Europe were as well prepared for it as the other; but this cannot be, till good shall have triumphed over evil in the struggles which are brooding, or shall have obtained such a predominance as to allay the conflict of opinions before it breaks into open war.

God in his mercy grant that it be so! If I looked to secondary causes alone, my fears would preponderate. But I conclude as I began, in firm reliance upon

Him who is the beginning and the end. Our sins are manifold, our danger is great, but His mercy is infinite.

Sir Thomas More.—Rest there in full faith. I leave you to your dreams; draw from them what comfort you can. And now, my friend, farewell

The look which he fixed on me, as he disappeared, was compassionate and thoughtful; it impressed me with a sad feeling, as if I were not to see him again till we should meet in the world of spirits.

CPSIA information can be obtained at www.ICGtesting.com
Printed in the USA
LVOW081950011111

253047LV00002B/147/A